MEN OF STEAM

BRITAIN'S LOCOMOTIVE ENGINEERS

L. A. SUMMERS

AMBERLEY

First published 2016

Amberley Publishing
The Hill, Stroud
Gloucestershire, GL5 4EP

www.amberley-books.com

British Library Cataloguing in Publication Data.
A catalogue record for this book is available from the British Library.

ISBN 978 1 4456 5605 2 (print)
ISBN 978 1 4456 5606 9 (ebook)

Typeset in 11.5pt on 15.5pt Sabon.
Typesetting and Origination by Amberley Publishing.
Printed in the UK.

Contents

Introduction

In Volume 82 (1938) of the *Railway Magazine*, there is a series of articles headed 'The Stirlings of the South Eastern: With some notes on the Cudworths.' Typical of the period, and indeed long after, this article is little more than a catalogue of the dimensions of locomotives built by the South Eastern Railway up till 1898. This kind of article could still be found in some publications in the late 1950s, and even afterwards. Yet those who, at this time, began to look at the overall picture and the personalities involved in locomotive design were not the first to do so. Long before, in his series of *Railway Magazine* articles entitled 'Locomotive and Train Working in the Latter Part of the 19th Century', Ernest Leopold Ahrons, writing between 1915 and 1926, compiled the most comprehensive coverage of all the ingredients of engine and train operation that was to appear until long after his death in 1927. Even allowing for the errors in these articles, we have reason to be eternally grateful for their republication in six volumes to which we can now turn for unrivalled information about Britain's railways, years before any of us were born; and also, to share Ahrons's wit.

Since the 1950s, more and more railway books have been published, not all of them reaching the standard of Ahrons and some of them, the further we get from the end of steam, doing little to advance knowledge about locomotive engineering. The example that really stands out is the RCTS history of GWR engines; we now have endless cut-and-paste jobs repeating, over and again, the original research by the team that compiled these books, even the unofficial boiler codes that were devised by those authors. Myths abound. Despite my definitively debunking the myth of the Hawksworth Pacific as long ago as the 1980s, it is still possible to find new books repeating the uncorroborated myths that have been published about this. The contretemps on the Midland in the years before 1914 have hardly ever been reassessed. Glowing accounts of the work of Bulleid and Gresley make no attempt to re-examine it. The contribution to engineering of James Stirling is lost in the fanfare for Patrick's 8-foot 4-2-2s. The contribution of Jane Stirling has long been forgotten, while Crampton, a truly significant loco engineer, is a prophet without honour in the country of his birth. By contrast, in France at one time, '*prendre le Crampton*' meant to travel by train.

There is actually nothing wrong with the use of secondary sources of information. Trawling original research can involve long and wearisome searches for documents that promise to reveal all but actually contain next to nothing. Not everyone has the time to undertake this kind of work, though they should attempt to do so. The point is that collecting reliable second-hand information should not involve repeating it without reassessment. The legend of Daniel Gooch tells how 'a brilliant engineer made ill-advised stipulations when he ordered locomotives for the GWR resulting in the almost complete failure of that railway and its eventual rescue by an unknown young man who created a brilliant victory out of chaos...' Maybe that is true but there is much more to Gooch than that. Gresley was knighted for introducing 100 mph speeds into booked train timings, and deserved it, but his overall career does not reflect that brilliance.

In this book I have not mentioned every class of locomotive introduced by the various men who form the subjects of this study. Those things are available elsewhere. What I have attempted – the premise of this book – is to examine the most important aspects of the life and work of the engineers who feature here in the context that 'no man is an island secure unto himself', and their work was affected by changing daily circumstances and myriad other matters – personality and family circumstances, financial constraints imposed by the Board, contemporary beliefs and attitudes, social mores and the living and working conditions of the times. I have already mentioned Jane Stirling. The fact that she was a woman has meant that her involvement has been rendered invisible by the supremacy upon which men insisted, even after women were 'given the vote'. The late H. A. L. Fisher wrote that, 'The fact of progress is written large on the page of history: but progress is not a law of nature. The ground gained by one generation can be lost by the next.' And this is no less true of Britain's railways. Steam locomotive improvement was clearly achieved but it was often cautious, sometimes regressive, while occasionally illuminated by sparkling brilliance. For that, the causation was as much outside factors as anything associated with design engineers.

In writing this book I have received help from several people and agencies to whom credit must be given; in no particular order and without reference to the nature of their assistance I would mention Leslie F. E. Coombs, Angela Gumbley. C. P. Atkins, Stuart McKay, Sam Bee (Fire Fly Trust), Peter Rance (Great Western Trust – GWT), Graham Watkins, Neil Burnell, Charlie Horan (PRR Historical Trust), Allan Halman (Hull & Barnsley Stockfund), Barbara Summers, Christina Black and Rainer Mertens (DB Museum, Nurnberg), and also the staffs of the Bodleian Library, Oxford, and of the NRM at York. Laurence Waters of GWT and Richard Casserley both gave significant assistance with illustrations of locomotives that were scrapped long before I had my first camera. I am grateful to Bob Green of the RCTS for permission to use Len Ward's diagram of the Crampton 4-4-0, *Falcon*. Also the *Railway Magazine* for the use, as a reference, of the photograph of Peter Drummond. The other drawings are my own renderings of diagrams that are available in the books quoted in the text. The portraits of the engineers whose careers I have described are creations of my own, usually based on readily available images. If there are others to whom acknowledgement should have been made but has not been, please accept my apologies; your contribution is much appreciated. For reasons of length I have been unable to include metric conversions for all the figures quoted. However, for those readers interested in those details I recommend the conversion app 'Units Plus', which provides a far more user-friendly service than anything that could be reproduced here.

Despite what is sometimes claimed, real history is no less scientific than any branch of physics, evidence being the key to both disciplines: it is an essential prerequisite to reaching the truth. The conclusions to which I have come are, I believe, supported by the facts. That does not mean that they are necessarily sacrosanct. After the reading of a paper to a learned society the members in attendance will launch into a discussion of the statement that has been placed before them. Put that in simple A-level form: 'The locomotives built for Britain's railways owed as much to the circumstances surrounding their construction as to the arbitrary authoritarianism of their designers. Discuss, giving examples in support of your contentions.'

L. A. Summers
October 2016
www.lasummers.co.uk

Chapter 1

In the Days of Daniel Gooch

The story of the broad gauge is well known: how a brilliant engineer made ill-advised stipulations when he ordered locomotives for the GWR, resulting in the almost complete failure of that railway and its eventual rescue by an unknown young man who created a brilliant victory out of chaos. In its essential ingredients the story passes muster but any detailed examination of the facts reveals serious blemishes on the gloss. Certainly the locomotives that Brunel ordered were the weirdest ever to run in Britain, and maybe the world. The design requirements set by Brunel were such that most of the manufacturers could predict in advance that they would be failures, though only Stephenson's were brave enough to ignore them. Two things are sometimes overlooked. The boilers of these engines were often perfectly successful; those from the strange articulated locomotives *Thunderer* and *Hurricane* were both used again after they were withdrawn in 1839. That from *Thunderer* was redeployed as a stationary installation and that from *Hurricane*, after being kept in the works for some ten years, was fitted to the freight 0-6-0 *Bacchus*, which ran for another twenty years. *Vulcan*, actually the first locomotive to be delivered to the GWR, converted to a tank engine, also gave twenty years' further service.[1]

It is often suggested that this nonsense was an almost unique oversight on Brunel's part, a civil engineer who was unfamiliar with mechanical engineering and temporarily allowed his attention to wander. Sadly that is not true. There are a good many examples of Brunel ignoring the facts or the advice he received from others.[2] The very concept of the broad gauge, brilliantly correct in its fundamental philosophy, was already doomed when Brunel insisted that it be used on the GWR. It was one thing to claim that 4 feet, 8½ inches was a colliery gauge unsuited for high-speed passenger traffic, quite another to be so myopic as to not realise that railways would become a national network with a requirement for inter-railway working. Furthermore a gauge of 7 feet and the complex design of the permanent way imposed demands for funding that only the kind of backers the GWR attracted could afford. Such funding would certainly not have been available after the 1870s, nor in the twentieth century. The ideal gauge was probably 5 feet, 3 inches or 5 feet, 6 inches, though neither the Irish, Russian, Spanish nor even the Australian broad gauge railways have ever fully exploited its potential.

There again, it was probably the Gauge War, as it became known, that created the legend of the truly great railway, on account of it standing up for its policies against the bullying tactics of its rivals. And let's be in no doubt of it, the behaviour of certain narrow gauge railways, the Midland in particular, was completely out of order. To deliberately cause difficulty in the transfer of goods and passengers from one railway to another was obstruction on a criminal scale, for which there was at the time scant legislation providing redress through the courts. It was this kind of trouble that evoked a rare interest in commercial operation by Parliament, who set up a Royal Commission of enquiry. This acknowledged the superiority of the broad gauge but ruled that the narrow was best suited to the country's interests. Hindsight strongly suggests that they were right and the broad gauge should have been abandoned there and then. But of course the Gauge Act 1846 was such a watered down version of the Report, with little real effectiveness, that Paddington could carry on much as before.

The opponents of the broad gauge must have had a good belly laugh when they saw the chaos created by Brunel's engines. Of course they attributed it to the gauge, which worried the financiers on the Board, but Brunel and the loco man he brought to the GWR knew differently and set out to prove it. That man was Daniel Gooch, as practical an engineer as Brunel was not and therefore well suited to understand where the other was going wrong. Gooch could be held up as a prime example of the Victorian dream, a man from the lower orders who, by dint of his own effort, hauled himself up to the highest level. Yet I am not sure that he would have agreed with that and not because he hailed from the lower middle class. Later in life Gooch kept a diary and also made notes about his early career. This reveals a degree of modesty and a willingness to go unrewarded for his efforts that is out of tune with the rags-to-riches Victorian. Yes, in later life, as Chairman of the GWR, he was voted huge sums of money by the Board but this rewarded a man who at the same time was declaring in his private writings that, 'The principle which has guided me through life has been a steady perseverance in the path of duty to my employers, not being disheartened by a first failure, but ever believing in the possibility of ultimate success...'[3] How different those words read to the prattlings of certain present-day individuals whose sole interest, whatever they may claim, is self-aggrandisement. At the same time the words may very well be a reflection on the career of his elder brother John, whose financial dealings read very disturbingly indeed.[4]

Daniel Gooch was born at Bedlington, Northumberland, in 1816. His parents were John Gooch, an iron founder, and his wife Anna Longbridge. There were ten children in the family, of whom four became railway engineers. His elder brother, Thomas Longridge Gooch, was engineer of the Manchester & Leeds Railway from 1831 to 1844, John junior was Locomotive Superintendent of the LSWR from 1841 to 1850, and there was also William Frederick Gooch. Somewhere Daniel relates one boyhood prank that very nearly went seriously wrong involved hanging another boy from a tree by a rope fitted with a slip knot. Something distracted their attention and they left him there, only realising later what they had done. Very fortunately he was not seriously hurt.[5] I think, if I had been that boy, I would have kept those Gooches at a good distance thereafter!

In 1831 Gooch *père* took his family to Tredegar, where he took up a position in the iron works. Daniel started his apprenticeship there under Thomas Ellis, who had been associated with Richard Trevithick's first steam-powered vehicles. At the age of eighteen he went to the Vulcan Foundry; here his experience was crucial: travelling with engines delivered to the Liverpool & Manchester Railway and meeting others involved in design and manufacture, he learnt a great deal that was useful, and which encouraged him to experiment, a trait that he never lost. Ill health, perhaps fortuitous, led him to Dundee and the Stirlings, and then, in 1836, back to Stephenson at Newcastle. Here he was employed drawing up the designs for two engines that had been ordered for a Russian railway on a 6 feet, 6 inch gauge. This was his first experience of a gauge wider than Stephenson's colliery gauge and he was impressed by the advantages that it provided. His next move was frustrated by commercial failure and another bout of bad health, meaning that he was next employed by his brother, John, engineer of the Manchester & Leeds. Thus it was that in July 1837 he applied to Brunel for employment on the GWR. His application was successful; yet this appointment was only one of the important events of his life to take place at this time. While at Stephenson's he met a young lady, Margaret Tanner, the daughter of a Sunderland ship owner, whom he married in 1838.

He confided to his diary that he believed his appointment was due to his firm belief in the broad gauge. This belief was real enough. He writes, 'I was not much pleased with the design of the engines ordered [by Brunel]. They had very small boilers and very large wheels...' *Thunderer* and *Hurricane* were

> immense affairs; the boilers were large, and the cylinders were, I think 16" diameter and about 2 feet stroke. In one the cylinders were coupled direct to the driving wheels which were 10' diameter and the other had a spur and pinion 3 – 1 with 6 feet wheels, making the wheel equal to 18'. I felt very uneasy about the working of these machines, feeling sure they would have enough to do to drive themselves along the road. As I said before I liked the gauge and the scope it gave for improving the engines but the designs of the engines then contracted for were bad.[6]

Getting them to work properly was a nightmare, as it involved many sleepless nights. We have a documented record of what happened in the reports of Brunel's Traffic Superintendent, Seymour Clarke, who reported daily to the Board.[7] Poor old Isaac Robson, whose usual engine was *Planet*, was driving *Vulcan* when it burst one of its tubes: '...he fainted off the engine at the Thames Junction while she was running. He struck against the bridge and injured his skull: this threw him back and he has a compound fracture of the leg.' Clarke reports another incident on 12 March: '...the 7 o'clock train down had gone as far as Ranelagh Bridge when the *Hurricane* and the carriages all got off in consequence of the switch from the Engine House being wrong.' Needless to say it was Gooch, not Brunel, who got the blame for all this, G. H. Gibbs declaring to his diary about 'the total unfitness of Gooch for his situation'.[8]

This was written on 28 December 1838. Others obviously recognised who was really responsible, for at almost the same time Gooch was asked to report, directly and not through Brunel, laying out the facts. An honest man, he did exactly that, reporting on 2 January and earning for his efforts 'an angry letter from Brunel'.[9] In fact the greater part of the report, while not ignoring the design implications, was about workmanship, which to our eyes, even allowing for the lack of heavy industrial experience, reads as serious deficiency. Brunel was big enough to understand that Gooch was right in what he wrote and it did not sour their relationship. Indeed, they worked together improving the performance of their best engine, the *North Star*. This had originally been ordered for the New Orleans Railway on a 5 foot, 6 inch gauge but was left on Stephenson's hands when that concern encountered financial difficulty. Originally intended to have 6 foot, 6 inch driving wheels, it was converted to the 7 foot gauge with 7 foot drivers; the cylinders were 16 inches × 16 inches.

It is interesting that the improvement devised by Brunel and Gooch involved altering the diameter of the blastpipe and positioning it concentrically to the chimney. Even at that early stage in locomotive development, the importance of blastpipe dimensions was being recognised. Gooch records in his diary that they also tried a blastpipe with the orifice shaped in the form of a cross.[10] It did not work to their satisfaction but one is perhaps entitled to comment that they could only have been a short distance, intellectually, from a multiple jet blastpipe.

Morning Star, a 6 foot, 6 inch version of the earlier engine, and nine further locomotives rooted in the same concept were ordered from Stephenson's and delivered between September 1839 and August 1841. Though known collectively as the Star class, there were significant differences between engines: all but the first two had Haycock fireboxes; some had domed boilers; others had the raised round top that became synonymous with the broad gauge. An amusing sidelight on early engines on all railways was the dumb buffers that were fitted generally until the 1850s. These were usually concertinaed cylinders filled with compacted horse hair. When the condition of the hair deteriorated and no one bothered to do anything about it, the buffers drooped, giving a cartoonish look to the engines. This could be seen on the GWS replica *Fire Fly* only recently when the front left buffer drooped noticeably; it has now been properly repacked.

During the period in which the Stars were being delivered and the fortunes of the GWR were, at last, improving, Gooch set out his own plans for a 7 foot passenger engine and a 6 foot freight type, both 2-2-2s. The most important factor in the success of these types was the grate area and the heating surface, the parts in which it can be argued that British locomotives generally were often wanting. Gooch recognised the importance of this factor for in 1844 he experimented with corrugated copper fireboxes on two engines in an attempt to increase the heating surface. He concluded that no advantage was accrued from fireboxes constructed in this way.[11] Note that the *Fire Fly* had a total heating surface of 699 sq. ft with a 13½ sq. ft grate and the Sun class had 607 sq. ft with a 12½ sq. ft grate, figures in excess of the generality of contemporary narrow gauge locos.

This, of course, was not all. Thin iron templates of 'those parts it was essential should be interchangeable' were supplied to manufacturers, who were required absolutely to conform to their requirements. Although a form of standardisation, this was not the system created by Churchward seventy years later. Just as Stirling was to do in later years, Gooch designed for current needs, and not with an eye on future requirements.

Against the date February 1841 Gooch wrote, 'By this time I was much more comfortable with regard to our engines... we could now calculate with some certainty, not only the speed they could run, but also upon their not breaking down upon the journey. We had no difficulty running at 60 mph with good loads.'[12] The narrow gauge companies' belly laughs were beginning to sound rather hollow now. Things came to a head in the Railway Mania year of 1845 with the promotion of many new railways, some no more than devices to outwit the other side, involving attack and counter-attack and reading like nothing so much as the script of a television drama.[13] The upshot was that Richard Cobden, acting for the narrow gauge interest, got Parliament to agree to the establishment of a Commission to decide whether the future expansion of the broad gauge should be permitted. It is not necessary to go into anything other than the broadest outline because the details are well known. As already noticed, the Fire Fly engines regularly ran at 60 mph. The narrow gauge engines demonstrated their capabilities on runs between York and Darlington. Two were provided, a brand new 2-2-2-0 long boiler locomotive built by Stephenson and a 2-2-2, No. 54, from the North Midland Railway. The Stephenson engine, known as 'engine A', was a very peculiar looking thing indeed, with 6 foot, 6 inch driving wheels, outside 15 inch × 24 inch cylinders and inside valves and frames. This ran out and back with a 50-ton train and then made one further run to Darlington with an 80-ton train. The best average speed it could manage with 80 tons was 43.5 mph and, with 50 tons, 47 mph. Several factors cloud these figures, including the claim that hot water was put into the tender tank before each run. More importantly, and characteristically of the long boiler type, the locomotive was very unsteady. Gooch rode on the engine on one occasion and afterwards cautioned Brunel not to do so.

Despite this, and like present-day legislators whose refusal still to accept evidence is astonishing, the achievements of the broad gauge counted for nothing to the narrow gauge side; they were adamant that their lines and engines were the best. Thus the directors of the GWR, now satisfied that Gooch knew what he was doing, instructed him to build a 'colossal' locomotive and this he did: the *Great Western*, the first of the Iron Duke class that set performance records that have become legendary. The narrow gauge could not possibly compete and it took them years to equal the best that these locomotives could do. The runs between Paddington and Didcot by *Great Britain* (with Michael Almond driving) were truly sensational.[14] Consider this: 1847 was only seventeen years after the opening of the Liverpool & Manchester, the first real passenger railway, and twenty-two after that of the Stockton & Darlington. Previously to that, even on the newly Macadamised roads, Post Office coaches still required sixteen hours to run from Bristol to London. The fastest known speed for a racehorse is just under 44 mph, achieved in the USA in 2008.[15] But note that the horse concerned, a thoroughbred, ran only two furlongs. The Arabian horse can outrun a thoroughbred for stamina any day but its average speed would not be more than about 15 mph. So a train that covered 53.1 miles at an average speed of 67 mph was outrunning the fastest transport previously available to man to an extraordinary degree.[16]

It is not an inappropriate digression to mention the Locomotive Act 1865, usually referred to as the Red Flag Act, by which road locomotives were required to operate at speeds of less than 4 mph in country districts and 2 mph in towns, and to be preceded by a man carrying a red flag. The claim that this was instigated by railway concerns worried about competition is complete nonsense. By that time rail speeds were far higher than was ever going to be possible even for powerful steam-powered road locomotives. It may, however, have originated with turnpike trusts, already failing seriously to maintain roads in good condition, as a way of restricting damage that they saw as emanating from the new steam road vehicles. This Act stands out as a dreadful piece of reactionary legislation in the midst of one of the most progressive periods in transport history. Had there been no such restriction, the development of powered road vehicles might have taken off much quicker and the establishment of a network of bus services feeding into the rail network might have become ancillary to, rather than competition for, rail transport.

Even Gooch's locomotives for the broad gauge were relatively primitive machines. The science of combustion was very basic; the performance of metals under various kinds of strain was largely unknown; knowledge of the effect of speed on stability was seriously faulty; and awareness of basic safety precautions was, to be polite, embryonic. Never forget that Brunel described the brakes on the GWR's original first class carriages as 'tolerably useless'.[17] Tell that to the Health and Safety Executive!

Accounting the responsibility for the achievements of the Iron Duke class entirely to Gooch commits the besetting British sin of rewarding brilliance but not its support team. Gooch was a practical man who learnt about engines from being on and around them and seeing the work of others. In this he was typical of his day. But we should pause and consider the contribution made by Thomas Crampton, who we shall meet again in the next chapter. Crampton came to Swindon in 1839 and was Gooch's Chief Draughtsman until 1844. Clearly this was several years before the original 'colossal' locomotive had been built (*Great Western*, 1846), yet the crucial design was actually *Fire Fly*, the detail of which was down to Crampton. The *Fire Fly* at Didcot Railway Centre is not a true replica, in that health and safety considerations and the fact that it will not be required to run at more than about 15 mph have meant that certain deviations from the original have been incorporated. However, beyond that, the crucial dimensions of the steam pipes have been retained. The collector pipe is 5 inches in diameter and that running from the regulator valve to the cylinders is 3 inches.[18] Thus we see, long before Sauvage or Chapelon, before they became general, large diameter steam pipes that, with the relatively high boiler heating surface, were the foundation of the success of these engines. Crampton went off to pursue his ideas elsewhere but Gooch did not forget what he had done. The boiler of *Great Western* was an enlarged version of those that had been fitted to the Fire Fly class and maintained the large diameter steam pipes, with nearly 2,000 sq. ft heating surface and a 21.6 sq. ft grate – massive dimensions for the time. It was to be another forty years before such figures became general.

Later versions of these locomotives had raised, round-topped fireboxes with four rather than two leading wheels. Strictly speaking, they were 2-2-2-2 because the Iron Dukes were rigid framed and not bogie engines. The reader may, if he is so minded, ruminate for days about whether this is strictly true, against the Webb double singles, which some would argue are real 2-2-2-2s. Excuse me, though, if I pass.

The historian is entitled to ask how much of GWR locomotive design of this period was the work of Gooch, given that the boilers were almost certainly the work of Crampton and that the frame and running gear layout derived directly from Stephenson practice. We have already noted that Gooch appreciated the opportunity that the broad gauge provided for improving the engines, and one of the elements of this was enlarging the boiler without any appreciable heightening of the centre of gravity. This was an important factor because the real causes of, and the solution to, the problem of oscillation caused by the motion of the reciprocating gear was not understood. At this time keeping the centre of gravity as low as possible had considerable currency as a solution to that problem. Remember also Brunel's avowed intention to pass the axles of his coaches through the saloons where the passengers were! Crampton's unique response to this constraint will be discussed in the next chapter.

Another member of Gooch's team, and one with whom he was on better terms, was Archibald Sturrock, who was works manager from 1841 until 1850. It is not often realised that Gooch had his office at Paddington, not Swindon, so, although he is indelibly associated with the establishment of Swindon Works, it was actually Sturrock who got the works organised and saw through the construction of the first locomotives. That Sturrock was actually an excellent manager and an unimpeachable support to Gooch is shown by the fact that the first 'colossal engine', *Great Western*, was completed in thirteen weeks from the order being placed and without complete drawings being available.[19] When circumstances more or less forced Sturrock to move on, Brunel gave him a first class testimonial and Gooch recorded in his diary his disappointment that 'Archie' had to go.[20]

Gooch, Crampton, Sturrock; this was the trio that I believe should be credited with designing and building the Great Western's early and highly successful locomotives. Straight catalogues of locomotives that used to be the mainstay of railway articles in magazines tend to omit interesting issues like that. Another, equally applicable to Gooch and Swindon, was the question of fuel. In 1842 Gooch carried out experiments with the use of turf as fuel and recorded that it 'was able to keep steam but required four times as much in capacity as the same result from coke'.[21] For many years there was much discontent about what was the best fuel for steam locomotives, usually coming down to the question of coal versus coke. The temperature at which coke can burn is very high indeed and the waste product is ash, not clinker. This very desirable property has an undesirable downside, because it is coal with the gas – volatile components – burned out. The refining process is expensive and makes coke use uneconomical in comparison with raw coal. I think we can assume that it was this question of cost that underlay Gooch's experiments with turf.

The first steam locomotives burned coal but they produced huge swathes of black smoke, provoking fury and outrage in communities forced to put up with it. Given that even modern steam locomotives can stain the sky dark grey, one marvels at just how unacceptable those early coal burners must have been. This is the origin of that misunderstood phrase in the rules for the Rainhill Trials requiring locomotives to 'consume their own smoke'. What was actually taking place was that the volatile components of the coal, best represented to the eye by the flames seen above it, were not being burned off because insufficient time to allow for this to happen was provided by the distance from the firebed to the tubes. The partially unburnt volatiles entering the tubes created the smoke and, worse, sooted up and blocked the tubes. The brick arch, devised as a means of lengthening the route from the firebed to the tubeplate, was first demonstrated in 1841 but it was not until the late 1850s that it became general.[22] Great Western engines continued to burn coke right up until about 1864 and, apart from his dalliance with turf, Gooch does not appear to have been an innovator in this area. It seems likely that his broad gauge engines were all coke burners and that coal burning fireboxes with brick arches were introduced by Joseph Armstrong. Definite information on the date and detail of this would be very welcome.

If the foregoing suggests that Gooch was not the progressive engineer that he is often credited with being, and I am not sure that he was, we might reconsider his reputation as an innovator. The old gab valve gears with which the first steam locomotives were fitted were inefficient, difficult to operate and liable to mishandling, causing breakdown. There were several kinds, some using one eccentric, others with two. The essential action was the moving of the eccentric(s) into forward or backward gabs connected to the valve spindle. With some forms of the gear, limited lap and lead was possible. Earlier versions of Stephenson's valve gear used gabs but the improvement devised by William Howe replaced the gabs with an expansion link that transformed the gear's effectiveness. The economic use of both coal and water was improved dramatically and Stephenson Link Motion remained one of the main gears used in locomotive construction right up to its last years. On the GWR, gab gear was used until 1847, the Iron Duke class being the first engines to have the Gooch valve gear.

It surprises many observers, as it surprised me, to have it pointed out that the Gooch gear was the invention of John, not Daniel, Gooch. The valve gear is the crucial element in steam locomotive design: get it wrong and all the boilers in the world will not compensate for it. Thus an engineer needs to be at the top of his game if he is going to start designing valve gears. On this basis it is fair to acknowledge that John Gooch stands with the best. Yet it is not irrelevant to ask why both brothers bothered with this version, given that the Stephenson gear was so good. Since Daniel makes no reference to it in the published version of his recollections[23] it is difficult to establish the likely facts. It is possible that it was a manoeuvre designed to avoid the rights payments that were due on the Stephenson/Howe patent. A much more likely reason accrues from the fact that Gooch differs significantly from Stephenson in that the expansion link faces the opposite direction and is stationary. The valve spindle connects via a rod to the die block, which is raised and lowered in the link. This certainly has an advantage in that it reduces the space taken up by the valve gear under the boiler and allows for it to be positioned lower in relation to the driving wheels, an important factor if the desideratum is to keep the centre of gravity low.

Armstrong persuaded Gooch to change over to Stephenson in 1862. This has long been regarded as an improvement, Holcroft stating, '[Gooch] has a constant lead whereas the lead of the Stephenson gear is variable and so results in a livelier performance…'[24] I am grateful to a correspondent for pointing out that this is not always an advantage:

> … as the cut-off was shortened so as to let the steam work expansively the values of the compression phase of the steam cycle placed significant stress on the relatively weak crank axles of the period. Gooch valve gear having a constant lead did not in itself eliminate the evils of excessive compression but went some way in significantly reducing this characteristic.[25]

The Gooch gear was never used again, at least not by the GWR. The interesting thing is it was used abroad, in Germany, France and Spain – in the latter case, on the French-built 0-6-0s originally intended for the Memphis, Pacific & El Paso RR, two of which ended up on the Norte Railway in 1879 and ran until the 1960s. No. 030 2110, *Perruca*, can be seen in the RENFE museum in Barcelona. On this engine the valve gear, eccentrics included, is placed outside the frames, allowing a full examination to be made of the Gooch layout.

Daniel Gooch also made a significant contribution to the testing of locomotives. Writing in his diaries with regard to trials with the narrow gauge companies he wrote[26],

> To enable me to [demonstrate the capabilities of the broad gauge] satisfactorily I felt a complete series of experiments was required, and having the authority of the Board to spend what was necessary, I designed and constructed an indicator to measure and accurately record the speed the train was moving, and also on the same paper to record the traction power used by the engine measured by a spring, also on the same paper the force and direction of the wind. To check the traction I also at the same time took indicator cards from the cylinder of the engine so as to accurately measure the power exerted there. It also gave me the power expended in moving the engines. I made a number of experiments over a level piece of line on the Bristol and Exeter line, at various speed and loads. They gave me results very different from those obtained by the narrow gauge, [which] however, were done more by calculation than actual experiment. I read a paper at the Institution of Civil Engineers on these experiments in 1848, and a good deal of discussion took place on them for a couple of nights. I still keep the records of these experiments. They cost me a vast amount of labour both in calculations and in making the experiments. It was rather a difficult task to sit on the buffer beam of the engine and take indicator cards at speeds of 60 mph.

And one might be excused for commenting that even behind a shelter doing this at 100 mph must have been interesting, to say the least.

Here Gooch is making the claim that he devised the apparatus for what has become known as the dynamometer car without significant assistance from anyone else. A claim has been made for Charles Babbage, the polymath mathematician associated with the early design of calculators. Babbage was certainly friendly with Brunel's father, Sir Marc, and introduced the son to the directors of the London & Birmingham Railway. But, despite this evidence of the Brunels being socially acquainted with Babbage, it proves nothing in respect of his having influenced the design of the dynamometer car. The obvious question is whether Gooch received assistance from the younger Brunel, a much more acceptable contention. Rolt's biography makes no mention of it and this is important.[27] Modern research, particularly by Adrian Vaughan,[28] shows that Rolt's biography is very selective; he has described it as 'hero worship' omitting a good deal of very relevant criticism of Brunel's work and attitude. Given this evidence we may, I contend, assume that, had Rolt been able to ascribe the dynamometer car to Brunel, he would have done so. That is not to say that Gooch did not discuss what he was proposing with IKB but there is no evidence even of that.

The dynamometer car was surely one of the most significant innovations made for the study of locomotives. James Watt established the figure representing a measurable and comparable rate of power as 'horse power' in the late eighteenth century. It is of course entirely unrelated to what a horse can actually do.[29] As has often been said, seeing 4,000 horses drawing a train out of King's Cross would be a sight to behold! But the point is that it provided a standard against which power output could be measured. The significance of the dynamometer car is that its equipment enabled several useful figures of performance to be accurately measured, among them of course the horsepower at the drawbar between the locomotive and train. However, the really valuable figure was that for air resistance to the train. Now, Philipson, writing 100 years later, is clear that there are several different origins for the resistance to a train's movement, not all of them finitely calculable.[30] Even so, experimentation that demonstrated that the resistance of the train at 60 mph was 25 lbs per ton of train weight was extraordinarily useful. As Gooch said, it was now possible to calculate timetables and point-to-point running times on the basis of known facts about the engine power required to achieve them. That by modern calculations the figures were not strictly accurate fades into irrelevance when it is born in mind that previously no such calculations were even possible.

A fundamentally important point is, of course, the ability to calibrate the equipment. The measurement of drawbar horsepower was collected via a spring placed between the engine tender and the dynamometer car. The spring had been calibrated to give readings on a scale of multiples of the power necessary to lift 33,000 lbs 1 foot in one minute. Unless that measurement was accurate, the results recorded in the car were worse than useless. And there has been more than one example in more modern times of inaccuracy being discovered after some supposedly significant reading has been made public. With modern technology the accurate calibration of load power measuring equipment is relatively simple compared to the primitive system that was available to engineers 175 years ago. That with such early instruments Gooch was able to make accurate results that can still be referenced today is surely what marks the significance of his work.

It might be argued that what he did thereafter was an anti-climax but I do not see that as being true. Certainly the locomotives built during the 1850s and early 1860s showed little if any advance on what had gone before. The financial difficulties in which many railways found themselves in those years hardly encouraged ordinary engineering progress; certainly nothing spectacular could have been achieved. Nonetheless progress was made in an area that Gooch could not have foreseen even ten years before. Against the backdrop of the frustrations described in the chapter on Sacré, Gooch became involved with one of the nineteenth century's greatest advances. Brunel usually had three or four, often more, projects going on at the same time; he did not confine himself to the requirements of the GWR as his successors largely did. His dreams reached reality also on the seas, with the steamships *Great Western*, *Great Britain* and later, the *Great Eastern*. The first two ships were built by the Great Western Steamship Company, the first in 1838, and the second finally, after much travail, in 1845, for the Atlantic passenger service. *Great Western* was a fairly conventional wooden-hulled paddle steamer but the *Great Britain* was a large, iron-hulled screw ship, the first ocean-going ship to be so built.

Flushed with the success of these ships Brunel, as usual, then went too far – dare one say, overboard – in the construction of a supposed super-ship for which successful power plants were unavailable and the requirements of normal trade not yet ready. The *Great Eastern* was a huge iron ship, so far ahead of its time that in terms of length and displacement it was only surpassed by the *Oceanic* in 1899 and the *Celtic* in 1901. It bankrupted its original owners and, shortly after Brunel's death, a new company took it over, operating a few trips across the Atlantic, including troop transits, until the mid-1860s when little work for it remained. It was then that it was bought from its owners at a quarter of its value by Gooch, who was instrumental in the establishment of a company to lay telegraph cables on the ocean bed. Gooch was by that time a very wealthy man, being a colliery owner and having owned shares in the *Great Eastern* as far back as 1860.[31] It suffices here to record that the great ship laid, in all, between 1866 and 1878, 30,000 miles of undersea telegraph cable between Europe and America and between India and Aden.

1868 was not a good year for Gooch; in that year Margaret, his wife of thirty years, died. His life was not without other tragedies, with one son dying at a very young age. However, in 1870 he married again, to Emily Burder, who supported him through the rest of life. Gooch had been elected Chairman of the GWR in 1865 and, though he tended to be conventional in his conduct in that position, there is no doubt that his general policy was very sound. His decision, taken almost as soon as he took the chair, to abandon the mad plan to build new carriage works at Oxford and instead to site them in the obvious place, at Swindon, is clear evidence of this. Obviously he remained interested in locomotive developments and may have been more involved than is thought in at least one new design. This was the near-mythical 4-2-4 express tank engine designed by William Dean and completed in 1881. This had side tanks the full length of the footplate from the cab forward and was mounted on two very poorly designed bogies. The full details will be found in my book on Swindon locomotives, in which it is made clear that the weight distribution over the front bogie was very bad, causing it to derail as soon as it left the works.[32] It never ran more than perhaps a few yards and was stored away from prying eyes under a tarp for three years. Gooch is said to have expressed to Dean his dislike of the design, especially the long tanks. Given that this reaction is not far short of obvious, one wonders at those who claim that Dean was a 'great' loco engineer.

Daniel Gooch died on 15 October 1889, having admitted that the final conversion of the broad gauge could not be long delayed but being saved by death from having to authorise it.

Chapter 2

The Crampton Inheritance

Because of the difficulty of discover reliable information, the figures may not always be strictly accurate. The available sources are often contradictory and the author has used those that he believes to be the most consistent.

There are two kinds of engineer: those who are best described as the 'steady-as-it-goes' fraternity, and those who seek to achieve radical advancement. Crampton was a radical innovator and the fact that in Britain he is still regarded as a failure is as inappropriate as its origin in engineering conservatism is obvious. That his basic design philosophy sprung from a misunderstanding that he shared with most other railway engineers does not alter the fact that several advanced features incorporated into his locomotives only became standard in Britain many years after his time. Despite several serious drawbacks to steam locomotive operation that were to remain obstacles to progress for many years, by the late 1840s railways had come to be accepted as the key form of transport in Britain, both for passengers and freight. Two of these constraints have already been discussed: the difficulty of devising an effective process for the burning of coal and the far more serious problem of the oscillation caused by the motion of the pistons setting up alternating forward and backwards thrust along the length of the locomotive. This tended to cause, in extreme cases, a motion akin to rolling, and poor and uneven track accentuated the enormity of the problem. As far as the locomotives themselves were concerned, engineers understood that the position of the cylinders was an important consideration in reducing this rolling or swaying movement. Placed inside, within the frames, under the smokebox, the rigidity of the locomotive tends to reduce the effect. Placed outside and further apart, the oscillation is naturally worse. The simple expedient of putting slabs of iron as balancing weights on the driving wheels was due to William Fernihough of the Eastern Counties Railway, who really ought to have patented the idea; it would have made him a multi-millionaire long before there were any.

The third significant problem with early locomotive design was securing better boiler efficiency and this tended to become linked with the need to overcome the oscillation problem. Bigger boilers, such as that on Gooch's *Iron Duke*, meant a higher centre of gravity and there was a belief for some time that it was this that caused the unsteadiness in their locomotives. Even after balance weights for the driving wheels had been adopted, several engineers sought to devise means of combining the two desiderata of improved boiler performance and a low centre of gravity. One such was Stephenson's long boiler locomotive: a longer, narrower boiler albeit with the same degree of heating surface, with the driving wheels ahead of the firebox, allowing unrestricted grate and ashpan design. Logic suggests that this should have been successful. Certainly Stephenson's idea caught on and many long boiler locomotives were built. Sadly logic was not born out by events; the long boiler locomotive was, certainly so far as fast passenger trains were concerned, a blind alley. The short wheelbase only accentuated the problem of undesirable engine movement and the long tube lengths actually reduced the efficiency of steam production. A rather different approach was adopted by Thomas Russel Crampton.

Crampton was born in Broadstairs, Kent, on 6 August 1816, little more than two weeks before Daniel Gooch, with whom he was to share his most important early work. His father was said to have been a plumber and an architect[1], which, if it is true, means that he was rather more than just an ordinary builder and pipe bender, for Thomas was privately educated away from the church schools that were the more usual way by which artisans' sons acquired their education, or perhaps didn't. He served an apprenticeship with John Hague of Cable Street, London. Exactly what Mr Hague did is unclear; in *Grace's Guides* he is credited with various ideas and with being awarded several patents as well as being 'for several years Chief Engineer to His Highness the Sultan of Constantinople'.[2,3] One authority claims that Crampton designed a steam-operated rolling mill at the age of 16[4]. Crampton went in 1839 from Hague to Swindon, where Westwood suggests that he and Gooch did not get on, the latter having a 'marked distaste for Crampton's ideas'. More worryingly, he adds 'perhaps because they were not his own, and threatened his position'.[5] I am not certain that I accept that comment. Certainly Gooch disliked Crampton's ideas but by this time his own position was much more secure, most assuredly with Brunel and also with the Board.

Mike Sharman dug deeply into the archives of the Patent Office and revealed that Crampton was devising new processes even while he was at Swindon.[6] Any dissonance with Gooch therefore arose from the possibly arrogant declaration of his ideas, which abraded against the more cautious Gooch. As we shall see, fifteen years later Crampton may have suffered for this discord.

During his time at Swindon, in 1841 Crampton married Louisa Hall, a singer said to have been a friend of Jenny Lind, who was known as the Swedish Nightingale, one of the nineteenth century's greatest opera sopranos. In 1841 two of Gooch's Fire Fly locomotives were delivered from G. & J. Rennie, and, perhaps as a result of this connection, in 1844 Crampton left Swindon to work for them. Of the brothers Rennie, George was more usually associated with mechanical engineering. As Chief Engineer of the Namur & Liége Railway from 1846, he was responsible for its locomotive stock and he seems to have been the first to be sufficiently emboldened by Crampton's ideas to put them to the test by the construction of a running example.

Crampton believed that the requirement to create bigger boilers, with much greater heating surface but without taking the centre of gravity too high, could be achieved by putting the large single driving wheel behind the firebox. He had previously considered putting the driving axle above the boiler – clearly not a sensible proposition because it defeated the objective of including a large boiler in any design. As everyone knows, the LNWR *Cornwall* was originally built in this form, and those who think that Crampton produced weird machines should, before commenting further, see the drawings of the early form of that engine. His next drawing shows a vertical boiler but this clearly did not permit the incorporation of one developing high power. There was also a peculiar twin engine ensemble that had the water carrier tender, in one direction, riding in front. Both 'engines' were driven and fired from a central platform, which meant that the fireman would be tasked with keeping both fireboxes filled from two fuel bunkers, one mounted on top of each of the fireboxes. Not a very practicable arrangement, though it might be termed a primitive form of the Fairlie engine.[7] In due course Crampton came to the general layout that we now associate with his name: the stern-wheeled locomotive that might, in Crampton's mind, have been instigated by early steam-powered ships. This featured a relatively large boiler, often oval in cross section, with larger diameter steam pipes and a narrow, longitudinally trapezoidal firebox. The latter, a most peculiar ingredient of a design radical enough in itself, appeared desirable because a normal length firebox would further lengthen the wheelbase.

There is still a good deal of general confusion surrounding the ordering, delivery and work of the first Cramptons. The first such locomotives to take the rails were probably those ordered by George Rennie, it seems via his own company, from Tulk & Ley for the Namur & Liége Railway, later part of Nord-Belge system, in 1846. *Namur*, completed in February 1847, ran trials on the southern division of the LNWR during that month. *Liége* must have followed shortly afterwards, though I have no exact note of its date. What exactly happened thereafter is not clear. The usually reliable David Bradley says that in April 1847 Crampton wrote to the Chairman of the LNWR offering *Namur* for sale because the opening of the N&L being delayed, the engine was not required. This being refused, the two engines ended up on the South Eastern Railway.[8] Certainly they were not delivered to Belgium immediately but spent some time in store. However, they were not the three engines Bradley quotes as being Nos 81, 83 and 85 on the SER. I think it more likely that Sharman is right to imply that they were eventually shipped to Belgium and worked there as originally intended.[9] For the purposes of this chapter it does not really matter. I want to examine, as far as possible, Crampton the man and his engines, and to follow their eventual development into mainstream locomotive design.

Namur and *Liége* were two of six basically similar locomotives built by Tulk & Ley, which can be described together. *Kinnaird* was No. 14 of the Dundee, Perth & Aberdeen Joint Railway while there were three additional machines delivered to the SER – actually the 81, 83 and 85 referred to earlier. They were 4-2-0 (or 2-2-2-0) inside framed types with 7 foot driving wheels and 16 inch × 20 inch cylinders, oval boilers with 989 sq. ft heating surface and 90 lbs boiler pressure. The oval boiler was necessitated by the desire to place it as low as practicable in the frame. The top of the dome contained a Salter safety valve and a second, with a scale attached, was placed on top of the firebox. The grate area is quoted at 14½ sq. ft, quite a large figure, but the shape of the box, with a surface heating area of only 62 sq. ft, strongly suggests that it was inadequate. The exhaust steam pipes from the cylinders ran forwards and entered the smokebox through cross-sectional extensions beyond the circumference of the boiler.

The position of the driving crew was not exactly enviable. Driven from the right hand side, there was a long, curved reversing lever with separate regulator rods. David Joy wrote, 'One rod being longer than the other, one shut off before the other; so she went "dot and go one" when nearly shut off.'[10] Across the front of the firebox, above the firehole door, was a large transverse spring attached to both driving wheel axleboxes; this was attached to a casting affixed to the firebox back. The length of the footplate was about 4 feet but its practicality was much reduced by the driving axle housing, which was at footplate level, with the transverse spring above. The possibility of some inadvertent jerk throwing the fireman against the spring just as it flexed is too horrible to contemplate.

Hamilton Ellis declared that *Namur* and *Liége* were 'extremely handsome engines' and then thinks twice about it before adding 'of an unconventional style of beauty'.[11] Given that most engines of this period had little to recommend them in the scales of beauty, we will allow him his opinion. As always, it is performance rather than appearance that counts. *Namur* was tried out on the southern division of the LNWR and is reported to have reached 51 mph on a goods and 62 mph with a passenger train. Details of its load on either occasion have not survived but it cannot have been very heavy. David Joy rode on the footplate during these trials and reported that it was a very rough rider. This is often related to the 'long rigid wheelbase'[12] but I am not certain that I accept the notion that this was any greater than was the norm. The wheel base of the *Namur* type, at 16 feet, was shorter than the rigid wheelbase on Gooch's Iron Duke and Waverley classes, which, though reported to run roughly, were not stigmatised because of it. And, compared to the Stephenson long boiler 2-2-2 type, notorious for its violent hunting motion, the Crampton was much to be preferred. The real problem of the lack of adhesion, due to insufficient weight on the driving axle, may not even have been evident in the early years when train weights were no more than about 50 to 75 tons.

Whatever was the general opinion of *Namur* it is clear that it made a satisfactory impression on the LNWR, for it now produced two Cramptons for its own use. At that time the LNWR operated as two almost autonomous railways, the result of uncompleted amalgamations. Locomotives for the southern division were ordered by James McConnel who, taking over from Edward Bury, set out to replace his predecessor's under-sized engines with those having much bigger boilers. The loco affairs of the northern division of the LNWR were administered by a shaky administration that was supposedly led by Francis Trevithick but in which Alexander Allan was the big wheel.

First out was the *Courier*, built at Crewe works for the northern division generally to Crampton's design but with certain Allan features, including an outside frame stay running from the cylinders to the rear buffer plank. Dimensions were generally similar to the *Namur* type but its appearance was different; the dome was of a conventional round-topped shape with a Salter valve on top. The firebox, of the same trapezoidal design, had its upper level raised 21 inches above the level of the boiler to take a second steam pipe in addition to that in the dome, necessitated by the tube area, which left insufficient steam space.[13] The usual transverse spring took the driving axle boxes. Gooch gear was provided though the set up was not particularly accessible. *Courier* is reported to have been unsuccessful but the reader is entitled to ask if that was just propaganda, Allan preferring his own designs.

The southern division was delivered of a Tulk & Ley Crampton at about the same time. This was the *London*. In appearance it was not much different to the *Namur* type but it was slightly bigger, with 8 foot driving wheels, 18 inch × 20 inch cylinders, 1,429 sq. ft heating surface and a grate area of 17.8 sq. ft with 100 lbs boiler pressure. Using Phillopson's formula,[14] that ratio of grate to firebox heating surface should be between 1:5 and 1:6.5; the firebox dimensions look much better but it is still trapezoidal in shape and therefore difficult to fire effectively. There were two driving wheel springs on long pins that perched them right near the top of the splasher on the footplate, where they were no less dangerous to the engine crew than in the previous arrangement. The engine weight was 25 tons 12 cwt and the driving axle scaled 11 tons 14 cwts. The remainder of the weight was taken by the carrying wheels, 8 tons 3 cwt on the leading wheel.[15] Hamilton Ellis says that *London* could maintain 'a mile a minute without effort over the magnificent easy grades of the old London and Birmingham line, with a train of about 50 tons tare, say 10 of the old four wheel coaches'.[16] Considering what we have been given to believe, this is a real hint that the Crampton locomotive was not the blind alley that has always been claimed.

A second southern division Crampton was the well-known 4-2-2-0 *Liverpool* constructed by Bury, Curtis & Kennedy in 1848. This was a much bigger engine than all those that had gone before, and is said to have been Crampton's demonstration that the power of the larger broad gauge locomotives could be matched on a standard gauge chassis.[17] If dimensions alone were the arbiter, then he was right. With 8 foot driving wheels, conventionally sprung, *Liverpool*'s dimensions, compared to the original

Iron Duke of 1847, were 18 inch × 24 inch cylinders (*Iron Duke* 18 × 24), 2,290 sq. ft heating surface (*ID* 1,945), 21½ sq. ft grate (*ID* 21.66) with 120 lbs boiler pressure (*ID* 100 lbs). In other words there was very little difference. The degree to which Crampton appears to be setting out to equal the Great Western engine can be seen from the important issue of adhesion; *Liverpool*'s overall weight was 35 tons with 12 tons on the driving axle, while *Iron Duke* weighed 35 tons 10 cwt and also had a driving axle weight of 12 tons. The frames on *Liverpool* were constructed to the double frame layout that he had patented in 1847: the carrying wheels and axle boxes were attached to long outside frames while the drivers had their bearings on the inside frames. In one form or another, particularly with the Jenny Lind type, this became a standard format on British railways, though not usually with outside cylinders.

On *Liverpool* the firebox shape was much better designed but there was still a section under the footplate that required some dexterous wrist movement to fill properly. A long mid feather divided the firebox longitudinally, requiring two grates and two firehole doors, a most inconvenient way for the fireman to work, getting in the way of the driver, as he must have done, to fire through the right-hand door. Such a large boiler hardly needed a dome and none was provided; the regulator valve was mounted in a box on the boiler and the steam pipes ran round the outside straight to the valve chest. These pipes were relatively large in diameter and, being direct, foreshadowed the idea of streamlined steam passages by several generations. Exhaust steam ran to the smokebox in the usual way, via a long straight pipe.

The reputation of *Liverpool* is that of a daring failure but I do wonder if that is entirely true. It spent the first months of its service working heavy trains between Euston and Wolverton and at some point was recorded reaching 79 mph. Referring again to Hamilton Ellis, he tells us that on the easy schedules of those years *Liverpool* had no difficulty hauling passenger trains comprising forty four-wheel coaches.[18] It spent much of 1851 at the Great Exhibition standing next to the GWR *Lord of the Isles*. Modern commentators tend to talk up the apparent differences in their appearance but I would deprecate this approach. The railway companies ran excursion trains so that 'ordinary people' could visit the exhibition, albeit on weekdays only; such people would, I think, marvel at the whole thing, not at engineering differences that even educated non-engineers of the day would have barely understood. After the exhibition closed *Liverpool* returned to the same work as it had operated previously.

Two serious drawbacks to this locomotive have been identified, of which the claim of poor adhesion may have had justification in some circumstances. Its supposed rival, the GWR *Iron Duke*, had a factor of adhesion of about 3.8, not a perfect figure but reasonable, even for a single wheeler. With its greater boiler pressure giving a higher tractive effort, *Liverpool*'s factor of adhesion was much more questionable, at 3.2. However, it remained at work until 1858.[19] This is very interesting. Another criticism flung at this locomotive was that it was very hard on the road, and in one ridiculous story that it had spread the track behind it. As Sharman remarks, if it did that how did its own train not derail?[20] If the 1858 scrapping date is correct, then it tells an inconvenient truth: whatever deficiencies there were in weight distribution, a locomotive that was a failure would not be kept in service on passenger trains for ten years. Ten years in service was not a bad term for any locomotive of those years anyway, and we can argue that it was with the increasing weight of LNWR trains that its only real deficiency became unavoidable. The possibility cannot be ruled out that *Liverpool* was as sinned against as itself sinning.

There are more than assumptions to feed that theory. If Crampton had not been on good terms with Gooch then the evidence is that this was pretty much general. His paper to the Institution of Mechanical Engineers[21] evoked an 'animated discussion, lasting over three evenings, … the opinions of English engineers of that day being distinctly against Mr. Crampton's innovations'.[22] There is some evidence that Crampton, sure of himself and his patents, had a tendency to arrogance and nothing disturbs the self-righteous more than the determination of the single-minded innovator. In his obituary it was stated that

> He invented endlessly, but few of his devices ever passed beyond the drawing stage. … J Foster-Petree observed that ideas came so fast that [he] was "incapable of learning from them". Early in his career he invented the Crampton valve gear, which seems never to have been used (probably because its inventor realised it was inferior to the Stephenson gear).[23,24]

I dare to suggest that, on this evidence, the lack of success attending Crampton's ideas was personal rather than resulting from any sustainable fault in his work. Among his inventions may be mentioned cast iron fortresses and a hydraulic tunnel-boring machine that put him in touch with Edward Watkin, the advocate of the Channel Tunnel. The essential element of this device, a range of rotary cutting discs that picked up chalk spoil and delivered it to a crusher, predated tunnel-boring machines designed by other engineers.

Crampton concerned himself with a variety of projects, not just in England but across Europe. This gave him an insight that many British engineers lacked. In 1851 his intervention saved from failure the project to lay down the first cross-Channel telegraph cable. With Sir Charles Fox he was involved with new water works in Berlin, and he was engineer on the Ottoman Railway line from Smyrna to Aidin[25] and the Varna & Rousse Railway. He was a contractor of the LC&DR and engineered the Swanley Junction–Sevenoaks, Faversham–Herne Bay, and Strood–Dover lines, the last including the 2 mile, 365 yard Shepherdswell Tunnel. He was later involved with Morton Peto and Edward Betts, whose fraudulent share dealings bankrupted not only the LCDR but Crampton himself. Happily he regained his reputation and was able to continue in business. The association with the LCDR and with Joseph Cubitt, its engineer, is important, for the latter actively supported and endorsed Crampton's proposals to its Board.

There is one other Crampton-derived locomotive that ought to be mentioned, E. B. Wilson's extraordinary 0-4-0 *Lablanche*, constructed in 1846 almost certainly without input from Crampton himself. It was an intermediate drive engine – that is, the motion drove on an intermediate shaft linked through a connecting rod to the driving wheels. To quote Sharman[26] about *Lablanche*: '[The] dummy crankshaft did not rotate, but produced a rocking motion. The centre of the outer cranks was set at 1'9" whereas the wheel crank throw was only 12". This meant that, while the drive shaft rocked, the wheel cranks rotated.' The mind boggles, though Hamilton Ellis[27] reported that it was said to have reached 75 mph, a claim that I find unbelievable. Apart from anything else it was clearly underboilered. Joy wrote that when running trials only his intervention prevented drivers screwing down the safety valve; but for that, the boiler would have 'blown her firebox crown out'.[28] Screwing down safety valves like this was quite common at the time. Needless to say, *Lablanche* was a failure; no one would buy it until it had been rebuilt as a conventional locomotive.

Apart from the two Belgian Cramptons, as far as foreign take-up of the stern wheel principle goes, it was in the USA, astonishing though it may seem, that the type first appeared. A 4-2-2-0 that Crampton called *Lightning*, designed in Britain but built by Edward Norris, was delivered to the Utica & Schenectady RR in 1849. Five 4-2-2-0 locomotives designed by Baldwin without any apparent input from Crampton ran on the Vermont Central, the Pennsylvania and the Hudson River railroads. They were typical American locomotives with bar frames, Bury firebox and Baldwin's patent 'half crank' axle in which the outer crank web was formed in the driving wheel itself, rather like that on an engine with outside valve gear.

Most fantastic of all the American stern wheelers were those designed by Isaac Dripps and Robert Stevens for the Camden & Amboy RR. Inspired by the British Cramptons, they were entirely locally devised and built, 6-2-0s with 8 foot driving wheels and 13 inch × 34 inch cylinders, the 3 foot, 2 inch boiler slung at an angle with the pitch roughly analogous with the centre line of the driving axle. The poor benighted fireman worked in what can only be called a pit between the driving wheels, feeding anthracite under the axle into the firebox. The driver had a great wooden cab that rose almost as high as the chimney and provided the usual forward door, but in this case allowing him to walk out over the top of the engine – hopefully not when it was in motion! Sometimes complaints about working conditions can be a touch excessive but the fireman especially would have been entirely justified in refusing to work on these locomotives. Against that, it should be noted that, at the time of their construction, southern railroads used slaves hired or rented from local slaveholders including women and children, labouring, cooking and doing other menial tasks. New Jersey abolished slavery long before but it is possible that the firemen on the C&A Cramptons were black rather than white 'engineers', the latter unwilling to accept working conditions that an ex-slave would have taken for granted.[29] Not surprisingly, the Dripps/Stevens 6-2-0s were failures and quickly converted to 4-4-0.[30]

It is unfortunate that considerations of space mean that only an outline of Crampton's influence in Europe can be recounted here. Readers are referred to the references for this chapter, where such details as have survived may be found. To a certain kind of British person, Continental locomotives were (are!) ugly monstrosities hewn with large runs of pipework and strange vertical cylinders. This antipathy may have originated in the appearance of the first French Cramptons and indeed may even have originated in British hubris at the fact that the Crampton locomotive was well appreciated in

France and Germany and much more successful there. Apart from the Belgian Cramptons, it was in France that they first ran. But, before outlining this important progression, the German position will be summarised.

Before 1871 there were nearly a dozen independent German-speaking states, of which eight had their own railway systems, which continued to be organised separately even though that of the Kingdom of Prussia was the largest and supposedly most dominant. A total of 135 Crampton type locomotives were built between 1852 and 1863, more than in France and more than three times as many as in Britain. The first were nine 2-2-2-0s, of which eight of similar design were built by Wohlert of Berlin and a further one, slightly larger, by Robert Stephenson & Co. for the East Prussian Railway (KPO) in 1852.[31] The best known are the Maffei locomotives built for the Bavarian Palantinate Railway (PB) in 1853 and the Badenia class, which ran on the Baden State Railway (BStB) from 1863. The Maffei engines were a batch of four 2-2-2-0s with 6 foot driving wheels and outside cylinders 14 inches × 24 inches. The design of the frames was rather complicated with the outside plates taking the bearings and motion, but with a large cut-out between the leading wheels through which the cylinders were bolted to an inside 'sandwich' plate. The steam chest was cast in one piece, in-board of the cylinders, and a heavy 'Y'-shaped steam pipe took exhaust steam to the blast pipe. This ensemble carried a domeless boiler with a very Stirling-like safety valve mounted on the raised firebox. The boiler was pressed to 93 lbs/sq. in. with a heating surface of 682 sq. ft, a conventional firebox providing a further 57 sq. ft, and a grate area of 10.5 sq. ft. Total weight was 28.5 tons. Because flexing of the frames damaged the underframe steam pipes, they were later rerouted above the wheels and subsequent locomotives, built from 1855 to 1864 by Kessler, were constructed in that form. Hamilton Ellis gives them a top speed of 75 mph.[32] Numbered 26–29, they were also named: *Konig Max*, *Hoho*, *Die Pzfalz* and *Konigen Marie*. They had all been scrapped by 1880 but a replica of *Die Pfalz*, as originally constructed, was built for the Reichsbahn in the 1920s.

The locomotive that has been at Nurnberg for at least thirty years is actually *Phoenix*, of the Baden Railway Badenia class built by Hauptwerkstatte-Karlsruhe for express train working on the upper Rhine valley line between Karlsruhe and Basel. There were eight of these engines, in some respects larger than the PB types but very similar in layout to the later versions, with a boiler-mounted regulator and steam pipes running directly around the boiler to the steam chest. The cylinders were 15⅞ inches × 22 inches, mounted on the outside frames and driving 6 foot, 11¾ inch wheels. The boiler was smaller than those on the Maffei engines, with higher pressure at 118 lbs, but 800 sq. ft heating surface and a more or less identical firebox, having a 60½ sq. ft heating surface with a 10½ sq. ft grate.[33] The *Phoenix* operated until 1903, in the last years acting as a shunting loco. During the Second World War, it was heavily damaged, but was restored in the late 1950s for the Nurnberg DB Museum. It is the sole surviving original Crampton locomotive in Germany.

It was the Nord Railway of France, partly British-owned, that took delivery of the first Cramptons to run in Continental Europe, in 1849. Jules Petiet was Chief Engineer of the Nord from 1845 and became Locomotive Engineer in 1848. Like many French engineers he was an intellectual who also held academic appointments. The Nord wanted something better than the Stephenson 2-2-2s and, probably through Petiet's awareness of Crampton's work, the stern wheeler locomotive made its appearance in France. The actual design is credited to the name of Houel, Chief Engineer of Derosne & Cail, who built the first and indeed many of France's Cramptons. The Nord series 122–133 were 2-2-2-0s mounted on double frames with 6 foot, 11 inch driving wheels and 16 inch × 22 inch cylinders. The domeless boilers had conventional flush-topped fireboxes with big grates and good heating surface. The exterior barrel was domeless with the regulator valve mounted in a box, with large diameter steam pipes running round the boiler to the outside cylinders. Chapelon provides a table in which the ratio between the cross section of these steam passages and the piston area at 1:8.4 was greater than any locomotive built until the arrival of the Nord compound 4-4-0s in 1892. He estimated their power output at about 400 hp, higher than most locomotives of their day.[34] They were everything that the Nord had looked for, regularly hauling 75 tons at average speeds of around 48 mph and reaching maxima of between 60 and 75 mph. Sharman reports that one of this series was recorded as reaching 93.8 mph running light.[35] The report is not well authenticated but, given the later exploit of the Est's *La Continent*, is probably within the realms of possibility. The Nord liked the Cail Cramptons and a further five series were built from 1853 to 1859, totalling fifty locomotives, most of which were generally the same.

The Paris Mediterranean Railway (later the PLM) took delivery of Cail-built Cramptons in 1853 but they did not last very long on this line, twenty being sold to the Est in 1869. It was on this railway that the Crampton stern wheeler's inheritance manifested itself most obviously. The Est Cramptons were in two identical series: Nos 79–90, built by Cail and delivered to the then Strasburg Railway in 1858, and Nos 174–188, built by Schneider in 1855. The appearance of the 2-2-2-os was originally more in line with the Nord types than those supplied to the PLM except that the boilers were circular in section, not ovoid. The original dimensions included 7 foot, 6¾ inch driving wheels, 16 inch × 22 inch cylinders, 988 sq. ft total heating surface, grate area of 13.34 sq. ft and a very high boiler pressure of 154 lbs. The driving wheels had heavy bosses over 3 feet in diameter, making the adhesive weight 12.4 tons against a total weight of about 27 tons and tractive effort of 8,200 lbs. This was later augmented by the fitting of iron slabs under the footplate. Train weights on the Est were around 75 tons and the Cramptons handled these trains with panache until 1878. No. 80 hauled the first Rapide express between Paris and Strasbourg. After 1878 the Cramptons continued in use on secondary trains for many years; they were withdrawn from service between 1910 and 1914.[36, 37, 38] By then they had been rebuilt with bigger domed boilers, cabs, sprung buffers and, later, with air brakes. All were originally named, the first series with geographic names like *La Globe*, *L'Asie* and *L'Afrique*. *La Continent*, the first Est Crampton, has been preserved in working order, having survived the Second World War on a plinth at the Gare de l'Est.

How involved Crampton was with the actual design and running of locomotives built in Europe in accordance with his ideas is not known. He retained an executive interest in affairs in England, as we know from his involvement with the London Chatham & Dover Railway and the SER. The three 'classic' Cramptons built for the SER in 1850 had defects that, when we recall the dimensions of the French locomotives, seem fairly obvious. The firebox was far too small with a grate area less than four times its surface heating area, boiler pressure was insufficient, and the adhesive weight was poor. Not surprisingly, they were very soon rebuilt with larger fireboxes and with heavy drag boxes below the footplate. They then gave useful service on lightly loaded trains until 1865.[39] Crampton was not popular with conventionally minded engineers but he does seem to have been able to 'sweet talk' directors into liking his ideas. The reaction to that observation is an obvious one but, again, it should be stressed that the experience of French and German railways make it clear that much of the opposition in Britain was little more than prejudice. Much more could have been achieved had the British-built locomotives had adequate fireboxes with more powerful boilers. The low adhesion weight was certainly a drawback but both the Continental railways and some operators in Britain countered this problem with slabs of iron under the footplate. It was clearly not irresolvable.

Continuing problems with driving axle failures, believed to be due to the effect of poor track, caused a return to the intermediate shaft drive layout seen in such early locomotives as *Puffing Billy*. Rather than direct attention to the effect of the piston thrusts on the crank axle as a likely cause of these problems, there was a sudden rush in the late 1840s to get out locomotives that incorporated an indirect drive. Crampton may have had a hand in this but certainly in 1849 he patented a design for an intermediate shaft located in the main frame half way between the inside cylinders and the driving wheels placed, as usual, behind the firebox.[40] Ten such locomotives were ordered by the SER from Robert Stephenson & Co. and delivered in the spring of 1851. No. 136, named *Folkestone*, was exhibited at the Great Exhibition and features in one of the earliest photographs ever taken of a railway locomotive. The 6 foot driving wheels had inside bearings but those for the four rigid (that is non-bogie – they had some side play) carrying wheels were placed in the long outside frame. The domeless boiler with flush conventional firebox had a total heating surface of 1,059 sq. ft. The grate area was 15 sq. ft. The interesting thing to observe here is that the cylinders are placed within the inside frames, driving onto the intermediate shaft, from which the connecting rod runs to the driving wheel crank within the double frame layout. It may have been thought that this was the best of both worlds: the longitudinal stability of inside cylinders married to an arrangement that reduced the stress of poor track on the driving axle. For myself, I cannot see that it was anything other than a conventional locomotive in which the effectiveness of the piston stroke was hindered by the interruption of its drive on the crank. Any advantage the Crampton principle might have had is almost completely lost. The Folkestone class were intended for express passenger work. They were actually preceded by the Bulldog class, intended for branch line work, with 4 foot, 6 inch driving wheels, built on the same principle but very different to the Folkstones. They were tank engines, which Bradley describes as 'Six coupled tanks with the centre pair of coupled wheels replaced by an intermediate shaft'[41], driven from inclined inside cylinders, the rear lower edge of which was very close to the ground. Not really surprisingly, they were later rebuilt as conventional 0-6-0s.

Events take a puzzling turn around this point in time; it is almost as though Crampton loses his way. With the LCDR engineer Joseph Cubitt supporting him – the 'Crampton-Cubitt mafiosa' as Sharman calls it[42] – he was able to design and organise the delivery in 1857/8 of six 4-4-0Ts known as the Sondes class and of the 4-4-0 Tiger class, much delayed, in 1861. They were very similar in appearance apart from the fact that the Sondes were saddle tanks with smaller dimensions. Two things stand out, the most important of which is that Crampton has, seemingly, abandoned his principal idea of getting the boiler as low in the frame as possible. Though the general layout of the cylinders and steam pipes is the same, with the outside cylinders immediately in front of the driving wheels, they are coupled and the rear pair are positioned beneath the firebox. The second point to note is that they were provided with very primitive bogies, centrally pivoted but without any sort of torque control, which could lead easily to derailment. The complaint against the Sondes class was that they were too powerful for the work they were intended to operate and also too costly in terms of coke and water use. Daniel Gooch was brought in to make a report and was scathing in his judgement.[43] Sorting out the bogie, as was later undertaken, would have made very reasonable locomotives of them, for I think that some of Gooch's criticisms could have been made of many contemporary types of locomotive.

Even before delivery of the Tiger class had started, when the problems with the Sondes were becoming apparent, Crampton was able to convince the Board, in the teeth of opposition from their own Locomotive Superintendent, William Martley, appointed in 1860, that his recommendation for further intermediate drive locomotives should be agreed. Martley was furious and there was something of a to-do about it.[44] In the end Stephenson delivered five 4-2-0 intermediate shaft locomotives during the spring of 1862. This was the Echo class and included the improbable but actual No. 30, *Flirt*. These were very different to the SER Folkestone class in two significant ways. Firstly the driving axle was under the firebox and driven from normally placed cylinders via the intermediate shaft. They also had the bogie fitted to the Sondes and Tiger classes. They were rebuilt in 1863/4 by the simple expedient of placing a driving wheel set in place of the intermediate shaft, making them into fairly conventional 4-4-0s; later reboilered, they actually remained in service until the early years of the twentieth century. The Sondes class, laid off in 1863, were rebuilt as 2-4-0Ts, dare I say, probably unnecessarily, in 1865. The same fate befell the Tigers, rebuilt as inside cylinder 2-4-0s between 1862 and 1865[45]. Inevitably the reader wants to know what was wrong with them. Hamilton Ellis suggested that the low boiler pressure was a significant factor, and the core of the success of the Continental Cramptons,[46] to which I would add the decently sized fireboxes. Though there were certainly problems with these classes, reports of accidents referred to poor track as often as any locomotive failing. The principal point is that, with a generous heating surface, high pressure, adequate fireboxes and large diameter steam passages, they were an example to just about every British railway then operating. Until they noticed what de Glehn and du Bousqet were doing, and for many engineers not even then, the example was ignored.

Not surprisingly, from the mid-1860s Crampton's involvement with loco design was minimal. His wife died on 16 March 1875 but he married again, to Elizabeth Werge on 25 August 1881. During the late 1880s his final essay was a double single 2-2-2-2 tank engine in which 2,000 gallons of water was enclosed in wrap-around tanks located below the level of the footplate.[47] These were cut away over the driving wheels and it appears that the cylinders, in pairs with their accompanying slide valves, rather than be mounted on the mainframe, may have been mounted on this tank. The cylinder groups were at opposite ends of the locomotive: that on the left side, mounted in a more or less normal position, drove the rear pair of 7 foot driving wheels, while that on the right side, mounted just ahead of the cab, drove the leading pair. The double cranks were set at 180 degrees, perfectly balanced on each side but prey to ending up all-in-line, which would have deadlocked engine movement. Transversely, the boiler was 'guitar' shaped with a corrugated firebox in the lower section and a combustion chamber and tubes above. This engine was indeed built but no record of its work exists.

Thomas Crampton died on 19 April 1888, very largely unappreciated, with his influence not recognised until much later. In the very year after his death, the Est Railway rebuilt former PLM No. 22 *La Belgique*, now No. 604, with a Flaman double boiler. This consisted of a barrel mounted above the normal boiler and firebox, with the crown of the firebox raised in an arch above it. As a result the firebox height was raised and the combustion space increased. The boiler barrel proper and half of the upper barrel comprised the water space with a 62.25 cu. ft steam space above. The 1,664.3 sq. ft tube heating surface was matched by 146.44 sq. ft in the firebox and a grate of 26 sq. ft. Larger cylinders, 19.68 inches × 25.98 inches, were fitted but apart from a cab the original Crampton 6 foot, 11 inch layout was retained.[48] The following year No. 604 was exhibited at the Paris International Exhibition and afterwards ran at 90 mph.[49] In general service, trains of 201.5 tons are quoted as being hauled at an average speed of 42.5 miles per hour over grades of about 1:150 with a fuel consumption of 41.7 lb per mile.[50] The success of No. 604 led directly to the construction of 4-4-0s with the Flaman double boiler in which the Crampton layout of the cylinders and outside drive on to the rear driving wheel is clearly evident. They were certainly not what James Stirling would have called 'bonny'[51] but they worked successfully for many years. Note also that the layout of the de Glehn compounds, as developed from 2-4-0 through 4-4-0 to the highly successful Atlantic types, replicated the essential Crampton layout, with the cylinders between the leading wheels and the coupled wheels and the outside valve gear driving on the rear coupled wheel. And the layout survived in French practice, where more than two cylinders was used until the 1940s. That was Crampton's real influence on locomotive design.

Chapter 3

The Case of Charles Reboul Sacré

This is a dreadful story, and its tragedy will be unfolded in the proper place. It is about a man who achieved great distinction in railway service, holding magnificent dual office; who was one of the most distinguished mechanical engineers of his day. Added to that, he was no mean economist. With such qualifications a man should rise high and Charles Reboul Sacre did so, as he deserved. But also he should stay high, reaping warm estimation and rich reward, eventually to meet his end in such tranquillity as mind and body would allow. This also he deserved.[1]

As a teenager in the late 1950s, my reading habits devolved into several categories: comic papers, of which the *Eagle* was the most favoured; novels from Tom Sawyer through Sherlock Holmes to C. S. Lewis's *Out of the Silent Planet*; and railway books loaned from the local library. The thrill of the blazing first paragraph or the twist-in-the-tail ending never left me, and so the words reproduced above took my attention as soon as I read them. Hamilton Ellis was a railway journalist who understood engineering but, more importantly, wrote some fiction and therefore knew how to weave a story. His story about Sacré was, and remains, all the more shocking because it was true; even after fifty years' research I cannot recall any greater tragedy than that which befell C. R. Sacré, Chief Engineer and Locomotive Superintendent of the Manchester, Sheffield & Lincolnshire Railway from 1858 until 1885.

In order to recall that tragedy I should first make it clear that my views are resolutely left wing, at the very least radical liberal, in that I believe strongly that the infrastructure that supports the economy should be publicly owned and operated for the benefit of wealth-creating organisations and the country as a whole, rather than be regarded as a 'business', the sole purpose of which is to maximize shareholder interest. Though they were joint stock companies owing nothing to anyone other than their shareholders,

Britain's old private railway companies were not, generally, marked by the same fraudulent misdeed that categorized some of the early American railways. Nonetheless, corruption was rife in certain sections of Britain's industries, as seen and recorded by Anthony Trollope in his novel *The Way We Live Now*.

My belief in public ownership of the national infrastructure is supported by this early railway history, particularly the career of George Hudson, the obvious example of a railway magnate interested solely in maximizing shareholders' and his own, mainly his own, wealth. The name of Edward Watkin is not far from that categorisation, the only difference between Hudson and Watkin being that the former was not squeamish about breaking the law while the latter observed scruples when it suited him. Watkin did serious financial damage to at least three of Britain's railways, inspiring opposition and determined resistance, and succeeding in creating a railway that should never have been built – all, and more, in the pursuit of near-megalomaniacal dreams. Amazingly, it is possible still to read descriptions of his work as 'foresighted' or 'visionary'.[2]

Two possible opportunities for the unwitting Sacré to avoid the ultimate tragedy came and went – one of his own volition, the other probably deploying him as a pawn in other's intrigues. The difficulties on the GWR after its amalgamation with the West Midland (WMR), and particularly when a former director, Richard Potter, became GWR Chairman, have been briefly referred to in the chapter on Gooch. This decided Gooch to leave the GWR and, according to Alan Peck,[3] on discussing this with Potter, he discovered that the former WMR directors wanted to appoint Sacré as his replacement. Gooch prevailed upon the old directors to prevent this going through and Armstrong was appointed instead. Peck says that Sacré had already been sounded out about this, but there is no evidence that this is true. More importantly, the question is why the West Midland faction should want Sacré as Locomotive Superintendent.

Watkin was among the WMR directors brought on to the Board of the GWR by its amalgamation with that company. He had spent an earlier stage of his life as the assistant to Captain Mark Huish of the LNWR, sniping at the GWR. In 1853 he had been appointed General Manager of the Manchester, Sheffield & Lincolnshire Railway and from 1864 was its Chairman. From 1856 he was a director of the Oxford, Worcester & Wolverhampton Railway, which became, as a result of amalgamation, the

WMR in 1860. At first relations between the West Midland and the GWR were not particularly good but, after difficult negotiations, matters settled down until there was a new and abrupt breakdown in their association. Just as abruptly, matters were patched up and the two companies amalgamated, with six WMR directors, including Watkin, joining the GWR Board.[4]

Exactly what part Watkin played in these intrigues is difficult to establish but knowing the man is to be sure that he was not inactive in pursing whatever suited his own interests. That the WMR directors became a faction on the GWR Board is clear enough; with Potter as Chairman, it obviously intended to be the tail that wagged the dog. Short of any authentic answer to the question, 'Why Sacré?' and given that Peck's story is true, it is not too speculative to suggest that this was a machination by the WM faction to infiltrate the departmental offices of the GWR. Since Sacré was both Locomotive Superintendent and engineer on the MS&L, the next step would have been to put him up for GWR Engineer when that position became vacant. Watkin's hand is clearly evident in these goings on. A further question is whether Sacré really was the pawn that this conjecture suggests.

He was the thirteenth son of John Joseph Berlot de Sacré, a several generation descendant of Huguenot refugees from Louis XIV's religious paranoia. Though English through and through, his French name may very well have been a disadvantage. France was the old enemy throughout much of the nineteenth century and fear of French invasion was very real, even in the 1880s and 90s. Hamilton Ellis describes Sacré as 'lively, intelligent, shrewd and hard working', but also as 'volatile and a practical joker'.[5] In 1846 he became a pupil of Sturrock, at that time still at Swindon. It seems likely that, on his move to the GNR in 1850, Sturrock took Sacré with him, as the apprenticeship would have been a personal engagement and not with the railway company. Thus, after completing his apprenticeship, he was appointed by Sturrock as assistant locomotive manager, first at the GNR's Boston works and afterwards at Peterborough. In 1859 he succeeded W. G. Craig as Chief Engineer and Locomotive Superintendent of the MS&L.[6]

The MS&L ran from west to east, through Lancashire, Cheshire, and south Yorkshire to the north Lincolnshire coast. Its main importance was as an adjunct to the GNR, which it joined at Retford and from which place MS&L locomotives took GNR trains through to Sheffield and Manchester.

Ahrons describes it as 'a plucky railway, having to overcome severe financial and physical conditions, and in Lancashire and South Yorkshire was frequently known as the Money Sunk and Lost'.[7] It had come into being as a result of the amalgamation of the Sheffield & Manchester Railway, which connected, end on, with the Great Grimsby & Sheffield Railway. It was also equal part-owner with the Midland and the GNR of the Cheshire Lines Committee's railways, providing an access into Liverpool. By arrangement with these companies, the MS&L provided all the locomotives required by CLC trains, except for some through Midland workings. The MS&L line was far from easy; I am going to quote Ahrons again, though he is quoting from a book published in 1884[8]:

> This is a route to breed energy. Of the 64.25 miles from Retford to Manchester, seven only are easier than 1 in 200. On such a route a journey speed of 35 miles per hour would be express. From Retford it rises 3.5 miles averaging 1 in 160; falls three more gently to Worksop; rises (two rests) seven miles averaging 1 in 150, and falls 3.5 miles averaging 1 in 120 to Woodhouse Junction; rises three miles 1 in 145 to Handsworth tunnel, and falls 2.5 miles averaging 1 in 150 into Sheffield. From Sheffield to Manchester it resembles the roof of a house, 18.5 miles of unbroken ascent averaging 1 in 125 to the east mouth of the Woodhead tunnel. 1,010 ft, followed by a drop of 22.5 miles averaging 1 in 145 (three easy) to Manchester.

I have quoted this in detail to give a picture of the locomotive requirements that resulted.

On taking over at Gorton, Sacré found immediately one result of financial stringency: an assortment of locomotives ranging through several wheel layouts; where they were designated into a class type, the number so nominated had few examples and were mostly inadequate to current demands. Sacré rebuilt many of Craig's locomotives with larger boilers and other modifications to improve their usefulness. More importantly, he put in hand several classes of robust 2-4-0s for passenger trains and the ubiquitous 0-6-0 for goods, some built by Beyer, Peacock, whose works were across the road from the MS&L at Gorton. Beyer, Peacock was obviously an influence on Sacré but so too was his previous master, Sturrock; most of his engines were double framed and in many of them the run of the footplate was raised over the outside axle boxes of the driving wheels. When Sturrock experimented with an early form of booster Sacré did the same, with equal lack of success.[9]

In one respect at least there was considerable difference between Sturrock's engines and those of Sacré. The former, probably from his Swindon experience, appreciated the value of high boiler pressure and adequate fireboxes. We should note that at this time there was a good deal of concern about the safety of high pressure vessels and it is said[10] that, when Sturrock left the GWR, Gooch told him to always understate locomotive boiler pressure. Since 150 lbs pressure became standard on the GNR under Sturrock, one might pointedly wonder about that. Like those of the GWR, Sturrock's fireboxes were also bigger than was general elsewhere. Sacré, on the other hand, used 130 lbs boiler pressure on most of his locomotives, and fireboxes that were more essentially of their time. Nonetheless his engines were good performers, as shall be noted.

In 1874 Sacré made a move to leave the MS&L. The reader will hear in his mind's ear the inexorable march of Holst's 'Saturn', subtitled 'The Bringer of Old Age', striding across his consciousness like the unstoppable force of mortality, which is what it is meant to represent. For Sacré that force was accelerated, and thus the looming tragedy, by his willingness to argue with Watkin. The Board of the MS&L, with Watkin as its Chairman from 1864, had by the early 1870s determined that it wanted a means of reaching London that was free of the restrictions that were imposed by its association with the GNR. For Watkin this was only part of the plan; the project involved building a new railway to the Continental loading gauge, linked with the Metropolitan and the South Eastern, and through the construction of a Channel tunnel, running trains direct from Manchester to Paris. Practical steps to bring this into being were at least ten years off but that allegiance between the MS&L, the Metropolitan and the SER was achieved through the fact that the Chairman of all three was none other than Watkin himself. Furthermore, the French Northern Railway (Nord), part-owned by the British Rothschilds, included Watkin among its Board members. It seems that Watkin discussed this project with his Chief Engineer and was not best pleased to discover that Sacré was opposed to it. Worse, he said so. The Chief Engineer favoured an attack on the north-east, a tunnel under the Humber giving access to NER territory. To Watkin the NER must have appeared like a gnat, to be brushed aside, unworthy of consideration against his vision of a pan-European railway empire.[11]

In 1874, therefore, Sacré applied to the London, Chatham & Dover for the Locomotive Superintendent's post, vacant through the death of William Martley. Now the LCDR is an interesting line, for its General Manager from 1861 and Chairman from 1873 to 1899 was John Staats Forbes, a former colleague of Watkin who, having fallen out with him, was one side of the appalling confrontation between the LCDR and the South Eastern for the cross-Channel traffic, which succeeded only in the near-bankrupting of both.[12] The reader will see easily how Watkin's intransigent determination on his own policies whipped up spirited opposition. At the same time, the opposition was maintained long after there was any sense in it, as both companies, after Watkin's death, came to recognise. So it is ironic that Sacré should attempt to move from a Watkin-dominated line to one that was in the forefront of opposition to him.

Sacré very nearly got the job. There were four applicants for the position; two were eliminated very quickly and the directors then saw Sacré and Kirtley again.[13] The ensuing tragedy was now set on its inexorable path by the appointment of Martley to the LCDR position. Inevitably the public records of the LCDR Board give no reason for this decision but it is no idle speculation to suggest that the crucial point was that Sacré was an officer of a Watkin railway; his loyalty may very well have been considered suspect. The decision, for whatever reason, was the first in a chain of events that, returning to the earlier musical reference, seem to have gathered momentum with the inevitability of the strident chords of Holst's 'Saturn'.

The MSL train braking system provided the next episode in this awful story. MSL trains had been using Newall's mechanical continuous brake since the 1850s and it was regarded as highly inadequate.[14] By the early 1860s brakes were still primitive, unreliable and chaotic, with each company using a different system incompatible with others.[15] The Board of Trade became involved and insisted that the railways undertake trials of the various systems then in use. The Westinghouse automatic air brake seemed to be the best but the automatic and non-automatic vacuum brake had certain advantages, of which simplicity of design was the most significant. Among these devices was the Smith non-automatic brake brought to Britain by the American J. Y. Smith, who was patronised by Watkin. Sacré reported to the Board in September 1875 that this Smith brake was working satisfactorily on the MSJ&A railway but that 'it must be remembered that trains on this line are seldom interfered with after once being made up … on our line however, it would be very different in many respects, the trains having to be broken up at various places and the speeds and gradients are very trying to machinery of this kind'.[16] The MSL carried out trials of its own and agreed with the GNR, who were already using it, to try the system on two of their trains. The work associated with this had hardly been completed when the GNR decided to follow the lead of the Metropolitan and SER in making it general on their trains. Fatally, the MSL followed suit.

The essential constraint to which Sacré was drawing attention was that on the Smith brake, not being automatic, if a coupling parted, the detached section of a train was not braked and would continue to move until its inertia expired. This was clearly extremely dangerous and, in 1881, in conjunction with the previously mentioned lines and several others, the MSL decided that the automatic system be fitted to all its locomotives. In fact it was five years before the MSL did anything to give effect to this decision.[17] The delay was due to the usual constraint, a lack of finance, to which the MSL was no stranger. The modern reader might break off here to demand to know why the railways continued to use safety systems that were clearly not fit for purpose, or indeed, why they were not compelled by law to adopt better equipment. I can only reply that it is the same philosophy that allows finance houses to pursue practices that threaten the well-being of the national economy; industry does not like to be regulated but history plainly shows the necessity of doing so. Hamilton Ellis says that Watkin insisted that Sacré adopt the Smith brake and everything suggests the accuracy of this assertion.[18]

By the middle of the 1870s increasing train loads made more powerful locomotives essential and in 1877 Sacré brought out the first of the two classes most often associated with his name, the 6B 4-4-0s. These had 6 foot, 3 inch driving wheels and 3 foot, 3 inch carrying wheels on an inside framed bogie that had no connection with the outside frame. The cylinders were 17 inches × 26 inches, the boiler pressure 140 lbs. The firebox was flush with the boiler and for the first time on the MSL, cabs for the engine crew were provided; they became a Sacré classic with a small oval 'port hole' window between the side sheet cut out, and the front of the cab. The layout of the frames was interesting. At first sight the 6Bs appear to be conventional double framed bogie 4-4-0s but this was not the case. The outside frames carried bearings for the driving wheels and continued to the front buffer beam purely as a decorative feature. Those inside had the bearings for the leading coupled axle only, a most odd arrangement. They also had big marine-type ends on the connecting rods.

These locomotives bore the brunt of MSL main line passenger work for many years, allocated to Gorton, Retford, Sheffield and Liverpool, from where they hauled cross country trains to Hull. Ahrons gives the 1880 timings for the 10.00 from Manchester (London Road) to Retford, which stopped at Penistone and Sheffield (4 minutes each stop) the 64.5 miles covered in 99 minutes net.[19] This does not appear terribly fast but remember Foxwell's assertion that, '... On such a route a journey speed of 35 miles per hour would be express.'[20] The highest point-to-point average was the 43.6 mph from Sheffield to Retford. On the other hand, the distances are not great: 28 miles 29 chains from London Road to Penistone, just under 13 to Sheffield and 23.5 from there to Retford; the allowance for the down grade Penistone to Sheffield section was certainly very liberal.[21] Bear in mind, however, that trains had to be started, accelerated and then slowed for station stops and, considering the brakes then available, these timings are not as poor as they seem – the maxima would be much higher.

I have seen no other reference to this but the reason for the peculiar arrangement of the driving wheel bearings on the 6B class may be associated with a problem that was becoming increasingly serious on railways generally: that of crank axle failures. The thrust forces from the connecting rod on the crank axle made essential a strong rigid casting that could be relied on to give continuing satisfactory service. Even in the 1940s, failure of crank axles was still regarded as serious and was a contributory factor to the decision by British Railways, at least at the outset, to restrict the Standard classes to two cylinder machines. In the mid-nineteenth century various expedients were tried to overcome this problem, deploying differing design of webs and the use of steel rather than iron. Failures of crank axles was a problem on the MSL and I suggest that Sacré's use of double axle boxes on the crank axle of his 6B class may have been an attempt to impart extra strength to it by providing greater cross support.

I also read a similar expedient in his class 14 2-2-2 locomotives, of which the first came out in 1882, seemingly reversing every aspect of his previous design. This had an interesting combination of inside frames and outside cylinders for the driving wheels but a double frame for the leading and trailing wheels. The cylinders were clad in a form of the Crewe/Allan set up, with an extension that became a crank housing attached to the driving wheel splasher. The marine big end was used again on this engine. The use of outside cylinders obviates the need for a divided crank axle because the crank can be cast integral with the driving wheel. However, to quote Ahrons, 'a large percentage of straight driving axles broke in service, so that adherents of outside cylinders gained no consolation from this'.[22] A factor that does not seem to have been considered was the nature of the Stephenson valve gear; the variable lead could have been a drawback in that it placed great strain on the crank axle.[23] I have seen no previous reference to this as being an additional cause of crank axle failure but it cannot be easily dismissed.

A further eleven class 14 2-2-2s were built in 1883 with some modifications to the outside framing and splasher boxes; in the latter case the replacing of the sheeted over splasher with one in which a spiral of openings radiated from the centre could hardly have been a sensible development. The GWR found that such splashers allowed men, carrying out some servicing task, to put their hands through into the spokes. If by any misadventure someone moved the engine, the man would very certainly have lost his hand. The 2-2-2s had 7 foot, 6 inch driving wheels and 3 foot, 8 inch carrying wheels. The weight on the driving axle was 17 tons 11 cwts, which Rouse Martin claimed was less than the real figure.[24] The cylinders were 17.5 inches × 26 inches; the boiler was pressed to 150 lbs/sq. ft, a new high for the MSL; and they had a 1,144 sq. ft heating surface. The grate area was 16.9 sq. ft. In general terms they were not large but 'for single engines they were remarkably powerful, they could get away in excellent fashion with very heavy trains'.[25] They gave good account of themselves on the line from Manchester to Liverpool for many years, taking trains of four or five twelve-wheeled carriages, about 84 tons. Speeds in the low 70s were sometimes recorded and those in the high 60s were common. At these speeds lateral unsteadiness was reported and this was put down to the relatively short wheelbase; much later, Robinson considered replacing the leading wheel with a bogie but this was never done.

As these engines began to show their paces, events were accelerating towards the final disaster. Sacré was clearly out of favour with Watkin and there seems little doubt that this continuing stress had an effect on his personality. He was on good terms with his enginemen and supported their demand for a shortening of their working day from twelve to ten hours.

Needless to say this was refused by the MSL Board.[26] At the same time he could not but be aware of the destitution evident not just on the streets of Gorton but in every industrial city in the country. Like many others he believed that a cause of this deprivation was drunkenness; for decades teetotal organisations have battled the 'demon drink' and Sacré added his support to the cause, unaware, apparently, like most other people, that drunkenness is a symptom, not a cause of destitution. It is suggested that he was depressed and, as a result, irritable and possibly short tempered with people who expected to be appeased. Almost certainly Watkin considered dismissing him. But he could not do that; Sacré's reputation was such that he could not have carried it off. For all that, he was in prime position for scapegoat when the opportunity arose. And it did.

On 16 July 1884, the 12.30 express from Manchester to Sheffield, consisting of a CLC horsebox, six coaches and three brake vans, headed by 6B 4-4-0 No. 434, with an experienced driver, accelerated down the gradient past Bullhouse signal box. Rounding the curve, the locomotive rolled violently, then spread the tracks and sat down upright between them. The horsebox was derailed but remained upright; the coupling and chains between it and the train having parted meant that the train, unbraked, ran into the curve and went over the embankment. Dow records that, once the terrible clamour of the train crashing down the embankment had subsided, the silence was broken by the crowing of a cockerel that had escaped from a box on the train.[27] A more macabre incident would be difficult to imagine. But for whom was this the cry of impending despair?

Twenty-four passengers were killed and thirty-three others injured. The retired engineer Massey Bromley was among the dead. Sacré visited the scene and was shocked by the devastation that he saw. Even in those days the public demanded to know what had caused the accident and who was responsible. The incident precipitating the accident was the failure of the outer web on the crank axle casting on No. 434. The axle had run 50,776 miles in service, having been fitted in May 1883. A minor flaw in the casting was discovered and this had clearly been the origin of the fracture. However, the inspecting officer concluded that this could not have been foreseen or prevented. The destruction of the train and the loss of life was due to the fact that the Smith brake had not stopped the train; 'a powerful continuous brake would have reduced the speed, with less fatal consequences'.[28] This unambiguous statement made Watkin vulnerable and he knew it. He had demanded that Sacré fit the Smith brake despite the concerns that his locomotive engineer had expressed. Four years before, the MSL board had decided to fit automatic continuous brakes, though nothing in that direction had been done. Watkin retaliated against the report by claiming that it was biased, basing this astonishing assertion on the fact that the former inspecting officer of the Board of Trade was now Chairman of the English Westinghouse Co.

Watkin's defence of the Smith brake can have been seen in two ways, the most obvious being his acceptance of the responsibility for its use, and indeed he was responsible. At the same time a reasoned reaction might have been that he was defending an executive officer who had made an ill-advised decision. Hamilton Ellis suggests that, while maintaining a neutral position towards Sacré, Watkin covertly suggested that his was the responsibility for the Penistone disaster.[29] The documentary evidence says nothing about Sacré's reaction to his Chairman's malevolence, yet it is not impossible that he too believed that he was responsible, not because of the brake debacle but because of the crank axle failure. We have already noted that broken driving axles were a problem on the MSL and the two design features that may have been introduced to counter it. The fact is that No. 434 had been received at Gorton with a flawed crank axle in 1883 and sent out with a replacement that also had a flaw in the casting. This, I believe, was the fundamental cause of Sacré's growing despondency, not Watkin's vicious failure to support him. What has been called the second Penistone accident was clearly not due to any failure on his part, but its originating incident can only have highlighted his sense of liability.

Less than a year later came another accident, again near Penistone. On the first day of 1885 an empty coal train from Ardwick to Kiverton Park was passing an excursion from Sheffield to Liverpool when an axle on a privately owned coal wagon broke. The wagon derailed, striking the locomotive of the excursion train, which flung it back. Rebounding, it hit the fourth coach of the excursion, which derailed. There still being no continuous brakes, the rest of the train pounded into the derailed coach and serious damage resulted. Four passengers were killed and forty-five injured, some of whom had to be cut out of the train. Again, no blame could accrue to Sacré for the condition of a wagon owned by another company. However, the accident report suggested that the MSL should institute better inspection of rolling stock, an implied criticism of the Locomotive Superintendent.

A third accident occurred at Penistone on 1 September 1886. At 21.15 a through coach to Huddersfield was detached from the 17.30 from King's Cross to Manchester London Road and left to await the arrival of the train to which it was to be attached. When it arrived the locomotive and brake van were detached to pick up this coach; returning to its train to recouple, the shunter failed to signal 'stop' to the driver soon enough. The lurch against the train set it in motion; six coaches, a dining car and a brake van ran back into a platform siding, colliding violently with the buffer stops. Twenty passengers were slightly hurt. This was just one more failure to set against the Smith brake. Sacré could take no more and tendered his resignation, which Watkin accepted. Sacré agreed to stay on as consulting engineer and thus put himself further at the mercy of Watkin's vindictiveness. Exactly who suggested this is not known, but why on earth he agreed to accept the consultancy is a question that will never be answered.

A much worse accident occurred just over a year later, on 16 September 1887. At Hexthorpe an MSL express from Liverpool and Manchester to Hull headed by 6B 4-4-0 No. 441, running at about 15 mph, crashed into the rear of a Midland excursion from Sheffield packed with passengers. The coaches of the excursion telescoped, killing twenty-five and injuring ninety-four of the passengers. This time the cause was simply the MSL engine crew not keeping sufficient watch ahead; as a result, they were charged with manslaughter. The accident could not possibly be laid at Sacré's door but the implication was clear: the engine crew had been long in his service and under his regulation, therefore he was responsible for their laxity. The connection was tenuous at best but Sacré's misery and self-loathing deepened. Watkin's masterstroke was to agree to accept all claims for liability, amounting to many thousands of pounds, which very nearly broke the company. If this appears magnanimous, it was nothing of the sort: it was his way of avoiding the cost of mounting a legal defence against the many claims that he knew the MSL was likely to face. It also dealt effectively with any questioning of the MSL's safety features, including that damned Smith brake system; by then of course the MSL was adopting continuous brakes, and not before time.

It seems not to have been any comfort to Sacré to know the truth about the responsibility for the introduction of the Smith brake. Even had he not been concerned about that, his other anxiety now struck again, not once but twice. On 15 July 1888, at Dewsnap Bridge, near Guide Bridge, the axle of a third class carriage broke and in the ensuing smash four passengers were killed and ten injured. At Penistone – that place again – on 30 March 1889 the fracture of the leading axle of 0-6-0 No. 188, hauling an excursion from Liverpool, Southport and Wigan to London, led to a derailment in which there was, mercifully, only one death, though the train was spread across both tracks.

The final straw was the Armagh rail disaster of 12 June 1889. A crowded Great Northern (I) Sunday School excursion was halted and divided near Armagh because the locomotive was not powerful enough to take the train up the 1:75/82 gradient to Dobbins Bridge Summit. The front portion was taken forward by the train engine but the rear section, now unbraked, ran backwards down the gradient into the path of a following train. Eighty people were killed and 260 injured, the worst railway disaster in Ireland and among the worst in the British Isles.[30] The point of course was that the employment of the Smith brake was directly responsible for the scale of the accident; had the rear part of the train been braked the accident would never have happened. The reader might wonder how Sacré could possibly have thought himself in any way responsible for what happened. But he clearly saw a link between its use by the GNR (I) and his acceptance of it for use on the MSL. It was too much to bear:

> He could no longer sleep as a man should, save by one expedient. Soon after half-past six in the morning of August 3rd, 1889, he rose and went into his bathroom. To the last he was an orderly man; the bathroom was a clean, austere place, and easily cleansed, whatever might happen therein; for with him he carried an old fashioned five chambered revolver. He put it to his right temple and pulled the trigger.[31]

Those words sent a shudder through the author when, not yet fifteen, he first read them. For Hamilton Ellis it was the end of the story but not for me, not now. The last words are with Longfellow: 'Whom the gods wish to destroy they first make mad.'[32] Watkin died in 1897, by which time the MSL London extension was under construction. The original route, end-on to the Metropolitan extension to Quainton Road, was opened in 1899; a new section, joint with the GWR, providing the latter with a shortened route to Birmingham came into being in 1903. Initially it provided an alternative way for travellers to London from the north-west but it never paid its way; was a millstone around the neck of the LNER; and was finally closed north of Aylesbury under the Beeching Report in 1966. Work on Watkin's Channel Tunnel started in 1881 and nearly 2 kilometres of tunnel were dug out before the British army, fearing a French invasion, persuaded the government to stop further work.[33] Perhaps the most extraordinary of Watkin's ideas was the Watkin Tower, a central attraction in a huge public amusement park near the Metropolitan Railway in north London. Clearly derived from the Eiffel Tower, work began in 1900 but the money ran out after it had reached the first level. It stood abandoned until 1907, when the demolition gang moved in. Tatlin's huge steel tower celebrating the Third International and the Bolshevik Revolution was never built. As an epilogue it fits Watkin's Tower equally well: that too should never have been built, nor the many other projects on which he squandered his associates' money, to say nothing of his ruthless determination, which ruined lives and caused the death of at least one great man.

Chapter 4

The Stirling family of Dundee

The Stirling family had long been established in the agricultural lowlands of Scotland when in the eighteenth century, at the beginning of the Industrial Revolution, Michael Stirling invented a threshing machine.[1] His grandson, James, born in 1799, became manager of the Dundee Foundry and later established his own business, in which his brother Robert, born 1790, became a partner. Robert was actually a preacher of the Church of Scotland and sometimes in trouble with the hierarchy over his advocacy of poorer people. If it seems strange that a cleric should also be an inventor then the reader should remember that it is only in the last fifty years that industry has turned its back on talented amateurs such as George Stephenson. In fact the 1876 obituary of James Stirling in the *Engineer* refers to his having been 'descended from a highly respectable farmer family, nearly every member of which, females included, possessed mechanical talent almost amounting to genius'.[2] And that is another interesting point. While amateur engineers from the ecclesiastical ranks were welcome to indulge their interest, the involvement of women in engineering is a very modern phenomena. I cannot call to mind the name of any woman who was even a workshop foreman on any British railway, though I would like to be informed to the contrary.

Unsurprisingly perhaps, given the comment in the *Engineer*,[3] Jane Stirling, Robert's daughter, did make such a contribution to her brothers' work, to Patrick's in particular. Shelter for the enginemen on steam locomotives became common only in the 1860s, and even later on some railways. This was partially a throw-back to the stagecoach, where the driver sat out in the open at the mercy of the elements and whatever nasties were kicked up by the horses' hooves; this last resulted in the provision, at the very least, of a dashboard to catch such items, but a driver's shelter never was provided, not even on the Hansom cabs that still plied the streets of London in the 1920s. Another reason was that the men themselves objected to spectacle plates and cabs, which they regarded as a requirement desired only by the unmanly.[4] Eventually, this attitude was overcome by the needs of simple safety; straining one's eyes through wind and rain, let alone engine smoke and sparks, was hardly a sensible way of driving an engine, hauling at speed a train carrying more than 100 passengers. It is said that, after the experience of driving one of her brother's engines and possibly suffering an unpleasant experience, Jane cut out cardboard and glued it together to construct a model of a cab for her brother's engines.[5] This was the origin of the Stirling cab, which, slightly modified over time, could still be seen on locomotives running in the late 1940s. Yet Jane remains unsung, a woman no less, in a world that men have dominated almost to the present day.

The Revd Robert Stirling's invention was the hot air engine in which energy is created by deploying an external heat source to warm the air in one end of a cylinder. James, his brother, was his assistant in developing the concept into a working reality that was adopted as the motive power at the Dundee Foundry and also in a local spinning mill. It was from this already celebrated family that the locomotive engineers Patrick, William, Robert junior and James Stirling came, the sons of the Revd Robert. Mathew was the son of Patrick, born in 1850. Their cousin was Archibald Sturrock, born in 1816. Patrick, born in 1820, later married and fathered four children including a daughter named Jane, clearly acknowledging her aunt. James Stirling's brood numbered five children, of whom the last was born in 1881, twenty-one years after his cousin Mathew. There were three girls in this family but none is known to have followed in their aunt's footsteps.[6] Robert Stirling junior became Locomotive Superintendent of the Anglo-Chilean Nitrate Railway and was instrumental in the development of the Meyer locomotive developed by Kitson.

The Stirlings came south to work on English railways, perpetuating the cliché that all engineers are Scotsmen. Not true of course but it is true that marine and locomotive engineering were professions in which many Scots excelled. Though the reality is that the proportion was probably no greater than that from any other area of the UK, engineering dominated in Scottish cities: Glasgow of course, along either bank of the Clyde, Dundee, Kilmarnock and New Lanark, to mention only a few. Engineering calls for very concentrated work requiring attention at the level of the smallest detail. The Scots' nature, particularly that of those from the west of the country, seems to suit this type of study, hence the apparent dominance of Scots in these professions.

The Dundee Foundry Company had been established by the elder James Stirling for the production of iron castings, Robert being a partner in the business.[7] Over the years its interests widened and facilities grew, to the point in the early 1830s when it was decided to enter the locomotive construction business. In lieu of real information as to the workshop equipment available, we can only assume that every locomotive was a one off job, even those intended to be of the same design. Most of the large components would be produced locally using cast or, where appropriate, wrought iron. The cost of wooden casting boxes could be reduced when they had multiple uses, say in more than one engine of a similar design. Boiler barrels were shrouded with wooden slats secured to the outer shell with encircling wrought iron bands. Boiler tubes may have been bought in; it is unlikely that there was a rolling mill at the Dundee Foundry. The strength of the boiler would be tested before fitting into the frames, hydraulically by pressing water to twice the intended boiler pressure, and then steam tested.

In those early years the wheels were not cast whole, as became the case later – they were built up from separate pieces requiring very skilled work over many man-hours. The spokes were cast individually with arrowhead formations at one end and a slot at the other that fitted into the rim. The arrowhead ends fitted together to form the boss of the wheel and had circular plates on either side, providing extra thickness and support for the welds. Additional strips might be welded between the spokes at the rim. Wrought iron tyres were affixed to this outer rim, usually through the simple but effective practice of cooling the red-hot, expanded tyre onto the wheel rim. Finally the locomotive would be assembled using a crane, the one big machine at the works, before a test run was undertaken. When locomotives were rebuilt or were even in the shops for routine maintenance, a wheel may have required refurbishment, replacement of a couple of spokes for instance. On those occasions the resulting wheel might very well look different to others on the same engine – it all depended on the foundry man employed to do the job!

Between fifteen and twenty locomotives were built at the Dundee Foundry from 1834 till about 1850, by which time it had been taken over by Gourlay, Mudie & Co. Young Patrick served his apprenticeship with his uncle in Dundee at the time that locomotives were being built for the Arbroath & Forfar Railway (A&BR), then using the 5 foot, 6 inch gauge.

These were 2-2-2s of two varieties, of contemporary appearance, with outside inclined cylinders and 4 foot, 6 inch and 5 foot, 6 inch driving wheels. Patrick may very well have superintended the assembly of these engines. In 1843 he moved to Napier, originally the designer and builder of marine engines, which, having taken over shipbuilding yards at Govan and Parkhead, began to construct its own ships.

In 1847 he returned to locomotive work as shop foreman at the Hyde Park works of Neilson & Company. He stayed there for four years before gaining new experiences in both marine and railway engineering. In 1851 he was Locomotive Superintendent of the Caledonian & Dumbartonshire Railway, which was a short but successful line connecting the steamers at Balloch Pier with the Clyde at Bowling. We have no information about its motive power and indeed Patrick was soon off to do more marine work with Laurence Hill at Port Glasgow, and then to R. W. Hawthorn at Newcastle. Hawthorns were building locomotives for the Glasgow & South Western Railway and it was probably through that connection that he obtained the post of Locomotive Superintendent of the G&SW in 1853.

Most accounts of the career of Patrick Stirling give attention mainly to the construction and work of his GNR 2-2-2 and 4-2-2 locomotives, regarded by at least one observer as the most beautiful engines ever built. His work on the G&SW is often passed over with just a short note but it deserves more attention than that. His main task at first was to establish the railway locomotive works at Kilmarnock, opened in 1856. Doubtless his varied experience of engineering workshops enabled him to undertake this task successfully; he was to do a very similar job in 1867 at Doncaster, upgrading the GNR workshops originally established in 1853. It is at this point that Patrick's younger brother, James, comes into the picture. His career to 1855 was different to Patrick's, who had been apprenticed at age fifteen to his uncle. James appears to have remained at school until aged eighteen (1853) and then spent two years with 'the village millwright', presumably in Galston where he was born.[8] In 1855, at the extraordinary age of twenty, he was 'apprenticed' to Patrick on the G&SW. Exactly what kind of apprenticeship this was is not clear, and indeed it was not until the completion of the new shops in 1856 that he was 'sent to Kilmarnock and passed through all the locomotive departments. On the completion of his apprenticeship he was made a charge-man, and subsequently worked in the drawing-office.'[9] Further experience was gained as a working fitter at the

Sharp Stewart works in Manchester before, just a year later, returning to Kilmarnock, eventually becoming Works Manager and, as such, his brother's assistant. Thus we see the same process that in those years characterised different generations of many railway families, sometimes involving sons apprenticed to fathers or uncles, or younger brothers attached to older siblings. James has suffered from comparison with Patrick's undoubtedly attractive and successful locomotives but his work deserves renewed consideration, for it was, arguably, more advanced than his brother's.

To return to Patrick, like few other locomotive engineers, it is possible to see him 'learning on the job'. Previous to the completion of the Kilmarnock workshops, G&SW locomotives were bought in from manufacturers, usually Neilsons or Hawthorn. There were four outside cylinder 2-2-2s built by Neilsons in 1855, four Crampton type 0-4-0s and two 0-6-0s with outside cylinders. Cabless and with domed boilers, they neither represented what was to become established as the 'Stirling type', nor were they much good. That Patrick was casting around for inspiration is shown by his approach to Beyer, Peacock for a locomotive with a Beattie boiler. Beattie was actually Locomotive Superintendent of the LSWR but had made an arrangement with BP for them to manufacture locomotives with his boiler, and Stirling's order was only one of several they received.[10] The locomotive named *Galloway* was a 2-2-2 with outside cylinders 16 inches × 22 inches, Allan straight link motion, 5 foot driving wheels and a total heating surface of 816 sq. ft.

The firebox on *Galloway* was a further attempt to make successful use of coal as a fuel. The G&SW engine seems to have been a half-way house to that end, with a double firebox divided by a mid-feather or water bridge. Let Hamilton Ellis, who was very fond of Beattie engines, describes the set-up:

> In *The Duke* [LSWR] of 1853 J Beattie installed his first coal burning firebox. It was a small one projecting outwards from the boiler backplate, discharging its combustive products into the main firebox, which contained an incandescent coke fire, as before, the idea being that the latter consumed the smoke [the tube-blocking volatile components] emitted by the former, on its way to the tubes.[11]

For all that, firing two different fuels must have made the fireman's life even harder than it already was; how many times, I wonder, did coal go in the coke box and vice versa! You can hear the fireman expostulate, 'Ach mahn, wit does it bluidy matter anyway?'!

Stirling did not use the Beattie firebox, though he used a mid-feather on his engines well into GNR days. More significant was his adoption of the general Beattie layout, the outside cylinders combined with the smokebox/saddle ensemble, with the leading wheel behind the cylinders and the fan of paddle box openings in the splashers. The Stirling domeless boiler first appeared on the Class 22 0-4-2 goods engines built from 1855, inspired not by Beattie but by domeless 2-2-2 locomotives supplied by Beyer, Peacock to the Edinburgh & Glasgow in 1856 on which the boilers were almost identical in appearance to the later Stirling type.[12]

Domeless parallel boilers appear to us to be the reverse of what we might expect to have been the natural process of development. A tall dome with a regulator valve mounted in it was a good safeguard against priming caused by water allowed to get past the regulator valve and into the cylinders. Stroudley once asked Patrick why he did not use domes and he replied that he would not tolerate having something resembling an upturned chamber pot on his engines![13] Yet it was not actually aesthetics that prompted him to run his boilers flush from the smokebox to the cab with just a brass safety valve mounted on the firebox. Domes were expensive to manufacture and it was considered that they cut the driver's forward vision. More importantly, he considered that, with the collection of steam through a horizontal collector pipe about 4½ inches in diameter and perforated at intervals with ⅝ inch holes running at the highest point of the steam space, he was collecting steam from the whole surface of the water and therefore minimising the local disturbance of the water by violent turbulence immediately below the opening of a dome, this effect being a factor in causing priming. A domeless boiler makes it essential that the water level does not encroach on the collector pipe but the jury is still out on whether this arrangement actually eradicated priming. In respect of the later GNR engines, K. H. Leech quotes a former shed foreman at Grantham during 1891 as telling him:

> In spite of no steam dome Stirling's engines were not given to priming. I remember at one time a signal box at Doncaster was newly painted white. A Great Eastern engine came along, priming badly and made a mess of the box. Old Stirling was stated to have smiled when he saw the mess, though he did not often smile, he generally just glared at one.[14]

Despite this, the only real advantage of what was called the 'straightback' boiler may have been that it obviated the necessity to cut a hole for the dome in the boiler barrel, something that other engineers also disliked doing, as it tended to weaken the strength of the pressurised boiler plates.

The first of Stirling's express engines for the G&SW to have these boilers were the class 40 and 45 2-2-2s built between 1860 and 1868. Class 40 had 6 foot, 6 inch driving wheels and 16 inch × 21 inch cylinders. Class 45 was an enlarged version having 7 foot, 1 inch driving wheels with 16 inch × 24 inch cylinders and 870 sq. ft heating surface. Boiler pressure was 125 lbs/sq in. They were good engines and, although not remaining on express trains for very long, worked until the 1880s, a very reasonable service life for the time. Ahrons wrote that the G&SW was not a line '... adapted to "singles"...' though he added that 'there always was the climb to New Cumnock ...[but] the old main line took a fairly level, though long detour via Paisley, which added some 10 miles in distance'.[15] The exact appearance of these locomotives is not absolutely certain and the illustration on page 11 of the image section has been drawn from various sources, including a very old and unsharp photograph. What is immediately striking is the obvious relationship to the 4-2-2s later built by Stirling for the Great Northern Railway. The components are not yet correctly proportioned but everything is there: flush domeless boiler with elegant brass safety valve, outswept smokebox side sheets attaching to the outside cylinders, paddle box fan for the driving wheel splasher and graceful curved rim covers for the trailing wheels.

According to David L. Smith,[16] Stirling was approached by the GNR to succeed his cousin Sturrock as Locomotive Superintendent but the GSWR Board attempted to retain him by making a substantial financial offer. Patrick declined this offer, which Smith suggests led to his 'ungracious' departure from Kilmarnock. James Stirling was appointed as his successor, initially for one year, later confirmed with a proper contract, which tends to suggest that any ill-feeling was very short-lived. The fact that James showed himself his brother's equal must also have softened attitudes. Patrick departed to the Great Northern before the order for his 7 foot 2-2-2s was completed and James supervised the delivery of the last in 1868.

There was fifteen years' difference in the birthdates of the Stirling brothers and while they shared certain ideas they were very different in their attitude towards other matters. Patrick has been described as an artist,[17, 18] a description that could never have been given to James; Patrick tended towards stasis in design, James displayed a greater willingness to make advancements; Patrick probably overstayed his welcome at Doncaster, still in harness at his death, while James left the South Eastern at the amalgamation of its operations with the London, Chatham & Dover and lived on for very nearly twenty years. This clearly contrasts with the Drummond brothers, whose life and work is detailed in a later chapter.

Anecdotes come best when they are spoken with an accent. Hence James's infamous remark about Churchward's engines, 'they are novel in shape, and expensive in construction but are certainly not "bonnie" to use a Scotch expression', loses some of its appeal translated into the pure English of an IoMechE Paper.[19] Just say it in middle-class, nineteenth-century Scots and the message comes over much better. That Churchward was irritated by this comment was not only due to the fact that he knew Stirling to be right, but also to the fact that James was hardly in a position to criticise. Cambell Highet describes the attitude of James to Patrick's 2-2-2s thus: '[he] had no use for the type and took the first opportunity he could of relegating them to secondary duties….'[20] He also rebuilt them with different boilers that discarded the outswept smokebox sidesheets and replaced the elegant brass safety valve with an open Ramsbottom valve mounted in the centre of the boiler. I can think of few boiler mountings, certainly on a British railway, that so disfigured a locomotive's appearance; yet he continued this practice almost without exception until the end of his time on the South Eastern.

Again in contrast to his elder brother, James was not averse to the use of coupled engines on express work, anathema to Patrick. The latter has been recorded as saying that a coupled engine at speed looked like: 'a laddie runnin' wi' his breeks doon'.[21] The implication is clear: Patrick believed that he could get the same power from a 4-2-2 as from a 4-4-0, a view that was not his alone at that time. The same belief underlined Dugald Drummond's early work and was instrumental in his double singles, put into service in 1897. James's first passenger engines were two classes of 2-4-0, the first, for express work, with 6 foot, 7 inch driving wheels, coming out in 1868 and the second, with 6 foot, 1 inch driving wheels, from 1870. They were very similar in appearance, using the same boiler with 861 sq. ft heating surface and 15 sq. ft grates. For goods work, over the years from 1870 to 1877 James built 0-4-2s, developed from his brother's similar engines, and progressively enlarged through three types. Although intended for goods work they were also used on passenger trains, leading to their being considered as 'mixed traffic engines'.

1870 was the year in which the first of Patrick's Great Northern 4-2-2s came out. Contrary to what is sometimes written, they were not an immediate success. L. T. C. Rolt for example, in his short length 'monograph', goes into ecstasies about them, hero worshipping, as was his wont, exalting about the mastery of design, but it is their appearance that he is complimenting, not their performance, which at first was disappointing.[22] They were made necessary by the increasing weights of trains, which were taxing the existing 2-2-2s to the limit.[23] On coming to the GNR, Stirling had jettisoned the Sturrock double frame layout and substituted inside frames and bearings for the driving wheels with outside framed bearings for the carrying wheels, the frame extended to form a valance along the length of the locomotive. This was actually a reversion from the outside cylinder layout of his G&SW single wheelers. I have been unable to find any definitive reason for this change though it seems to me obvious enough, even aside from any consideration of appearance. The leading wheel on the Glasgow single wheelers was behind the cylinders and it seems likely that the action of the piston must have caused oscillation in the form of rolling, particularly at high speed. With the cylinders placed inside the frames over the leading axle, this oscillation was very much reduced.

The first 2-2-2 came out in 1868 and the last as late as 1894 in six basic types, the first with 7 foot, 1 inch driving wheels and those built after 1870 with 7 foot, 7½ inch wheels. The first 7 foot, 7 inch engine was No. 92, which reused the driving wheels from the Sturrock 4-2-2 No. 215, withdrawn in 1870. The wheels were considered suitable for further work and with new tyres they gave further service until 1883, when No. 92 was rebuilt with a slightly larger boiler and new driving wheels with the diameter increased by half an inch. No. 92 was described as being 'the swiftest engine that ever ran on Great Northern metals' and this clearly encouraged construction of more 2-2-2s with the larger drivers. Ahrons has said that, despite being relatively small engines, they could do very good work[24] and this tends to be confirmed by reports that there was little to choose between the later, larger 2-2-2s and the bogie singles. Given that the last 2-2-2s had the same boilers as the 4-2-2s, this is not as surprising as might be thought. Interchangability of boilers, cylinders and motion was a feature of Patrick Stirling's work but this was not standardisation in the twentieth-century form. Stirling's boilers were designed for current needs. Leech and Boddy say that 'the single wheelers were regarded as special engines for their own particular and more arduous work, and that while the odd standard parts were conveniently used, there was no attempt to cramp the proportions of the design merely for the sake of standardisation'.[25] It has been said that the Board did not encourage him to consider future requirements; thus, by 1895 his engines were adequate but no more. Another equally serious problem was the very poor GNR track, which necessitated low axle loads, meaning boilers with something in reserve, necessarily heavier, were not really possible.[26]

We are getting ahead of ourselves but it is not inappropriate at this point to note the figures quoted by Leech & Boddy, which indicate the results of the Board's unwillingness to invest and Stirling's effective leadership.[27] In 1866 there were about 400 engines on the GNR earning around £4,600 each per year; by 1873 this figure was £5,600 per engine, a significant improvement given the low inflation of those years. Overall maintenance and renewal cost just over 3*d* per train mile. The coal consumption of the 7 foot singles was given as 21 lb/mile in 1868 and in 1885 Stirling reported that on bogie single No. 771, working the Sheffield–London expresses, careful testing with trains weighing 75 and 87 tons showed that the heavier but slower train burnt 19.4 lbs/mile but the lighter but faster 22.2 lbs/mile.[28] On this he commented that it showed 'how expensively increased speed is obtained'. Further trials in 1881 with an NER 2-4-0 compound gave the Great Northern the better of it, though the GNR footplate men probably rose to the occasion by doing their best to keep the coal use as low as possible. This raises the point that all economy-seeking operators should understand: engineers can provide their locomotives with all the cost-saving devices possible, including improved methods of operation, but if the enginemen will not take advantage of them, no savings will accrue.

GNR 4-2-2 No. 1 was delivered in 1870. For some months it was the only member of its class, in the circumstances a sensible caution. To achieve greater hauling power, Stirling considered that greater adhesion weight was necessary, hence the decision to use 8 foot driving wheels (actually 8 foot, 1 inch), which, with Stirling's desire to keep the boiler pitch low for aesthetic reasons, and also to maintain a lower centre of gravity, made outside cylinders unavoidable. While Stirling might have preferred for the engine to be a 2-2-2, experience with the unwieldy front end of the outside cylindered 2-2-2s on the G&SW made the use of a front bogie unavoidable.

4-2-2 No. 1 in its original condition was under boilered, the firebox was not big enough and the heating surface totalling little more than 1,000 sq. ft was insufficient. The firebox was provided with a mid-feather rather than a brick arch. Notice the importance of the blastpipe again; the very tall exhaust pipe had to be reduced by 5 inches to improve the draught. The original slide valves were troublesome. Originally it was not fitted with brakes, but that was a standard feature of early Stirling engines and should not be viewed out of context. The bogie was pivoted 6 inches behind its centre line, meaning that greater weight was carried at the front. Stirling said that this meant that the bogie was 'leading the driving wheels'. These teething troubles were a source of much concern in the Locomotive Superintendent's office. Indeed, the 4-4-0 drawing discovered long afterwards, signed by J. C. Park, Stirling's Chief Draughtsman, may actually have been a suggestion for an alternative design. If this was the case then Stirling gave it short shrift; experience with some 2-4-0s later rebuilt as 2-2-2s confirmed in him his dislike of coupled wheels for express locomotives. Leech and Boddy say that he would never have reacted to problems with a design by devising an entirely new one.[29] Is it unfair to contrast this with E. S. Cox's comment on Stanier that 'he would never seek to cover up bad engineering by worse'?[30] The problem for Stirling is that he was constrained by the Board's parsimony with money. Orders for locomotives were only for small batches; although there were eventually fifty-three 4-2-2s, the last was not running until 1895. There was just not the funding for new types of locomotive – what you had was what you had to make work.

It is unlikely that these teething troubles were serious; in its first eight months' work, No. 1 ran 32,000 miles – making allowances for boiler washouts and so forth, perhaps 160 miles a day. More to the point would be comparative figures, more specific than those already quoted, for coal use by this first engine. Adequate performance looks very different when considerations of this kind are in focus. When the second 8-footer, No. 8, came out it had a new design of boiler with a greater heating surface and much larger firebox. To accommodate this, the main frame and wheel base were lengthened. No. 8 and the third example, No. 33, retained the mid feather design but a brick arch was used in all subsequent members of the class and the three earliest were converted to suit. Between 1870 and 1882 thirty-seven 4-2-2s were built. Between 1884 and 1893 a further ten came out with driving wheels increased by ½ inch, trailing wheels by 6½ inches and boiler pressure increased to 160 lbs. The spring safety valve was also replaced by a Ramsbottom lock-up type, still contained within the curvaceous brass bonnet.

In the 1888 Race to the North, the GNR was represented by engines of both the 2-2-2 and 8-footer classes, the interesting point being that there was not a great deal to choose between the performance of either. Stirling's account of the works of these engines can be read in the *Engineer*.[31] They show that average speeds over both the section between King's Cross and Grantham and Grantham and York were generally between about 54 and 60 mph, with the fastest reaching 61.2 on the more northerly run shortly before the competition was called off. The fastest incidental speed was around 70 mph. Writing in 1915, Ahrons records a run that he describes as representational, with 4-2-2 No. 773, one of this second batch, taking a 90-ton train from Grantham to King's Cross, in which he records the passing times and speeds at every mile post.[32] Getting away from Grantham, the engine was wound up to 60 mph just past Stoke Summit and allowed to descend to Peterborough at high speed; 72 was achieved at MP 93 and 75 three miles later. Beyond MP 86 speed was reduced but remained over 60 mph for 7 miles until slowing for the Peterborough slack brought it right down. Beyond Peterborough No. 773 had time in hand and was held to what was demanded by the booked timing. The pass-to-pass average from MP 98 to MP 8 was 57.1 mph.

By 1888 brother James was well ensconced at Ashford as Locomotive Superintendent of the South Eastern Railway. Evidence that he had a rather different approach to Patrick had already burst upon the world with his first engines for the G&SW, 2-4-0 express engines. In 1873 a real break occurred when the first of the Class 6 4-4-0s came out, described by Ahrons as 'probably the most celebrated express engines that ever ran on the [G&SW]'.[33] Apart from the smaller 4-4-0s built by Wheatley for the NBR in 1871, these were the first British inside cylinder bogie 4-4-0s and, inasmuch that they were somewhat better performers than the NBR engines, ought perhaps to be regarded as the great progenitors of that long-lived type.[34] With 7 foot, 1 inch driving wheels, 18 inch × 26 inch cylinders, heating surface at 1,111 sq. ft and boiler pressure of 140 lbs with a 16 sq. ft grate, these engines were larger than GNR 8-footer No. 1 and not eclipsed by Nos 8 or 33 either. Steam reversing gear was introduced with the second member of the class, later becoming standard and taken by James to the SER.

As far as appearance goes, they were obviously Stirling family products, with fan-shaped openings in the splashers and, set out from them above the level of the running board, long skirting plates with semi-circular openings to access the coupling rod bushes. Both brothers had used the fitting on their 2-4-0s but who initiated it I am not certain. The boilers were James's version of the straight back boiler but with the lock up safety valves mounted, unshrouded, on the firebox. This deviation from James's normal practice of putting it on the middle ring of the boiler, in the position usually occupied by the dome is rather puzzling. More extraordinary is that Smellie,[35] who largely copied the Stirling format, built 4-4-0s with the safety valve on the boiler. Six of the Class 6 engines had been withdrawn when Manson intervened to rebuild the surviving sixteen into the 194 class with his own form of cab and chimney but with Smellie boilers, thus restoring the traditional Stirling appearance. The last ran until 1930.

The original impetus to build the Class 6 had been the completion of the Midland Railway's line to Carlisle from Settle, built in direct competition with the LNWR, and its wish to see its trains taken on to Glasgow by a company other than the North Western's Caledonian ally. The Midland took their expresses from St Pancras as far as Carlisle where the G&SW 4-4-0s took the trains on to St Enoch. The load was usually one Pullman car, one or two twelve-wheeled bogies and five or six six-wheeled coaches plus two vans – say 150 tons.[36] Double heading was usually employed on the stiffest section between Dumfries and Kilmarnock, 58.25 miles involving the New Cumnock gradient, 35 miles at 1:150 to 1:200. The scheduled average speeds were 47.15mph between Carlisle and Dumfries, 44.8 mph to Kilmarnock and 41.6 mph thence to St Enoch.[37] Overall this was not bad running and G&SW enginemen were very attached to the 'auld bogies'.

Much to everyone's surprise, James Stirling left the G&SW in 1878 to go to the South Eastern and never returned. At Ashford he found a company in what can only be called serious straits. Deep into the warfare with its detested rival the London, Chatham & Dover and ruled with iron by the same Edward Watkin who was largely responsible for Sacré's suicide, its Locomotive Superintendent James Cudworth had fallen out with Watkin and departed the place, leaving mechanical engineering to be shared by Watkin's son Alfred and the Ashford works manager, Richard Mansell. The latter is best known as the originator of the wooden wheel centre named after him. Having the boss's son run a department could never have satisfied Ashford's engineers or been acceptable to the workforce, not that the latter would have kept Watkin awake at night. The appointment of James Stirling was, therefore, fortuitous in that his reputation, based on the G&SW 4-4-0s, gave him an initial advantage with the locomotive department, thus starting to repair the damage caused in the first place by Cudworth's disinclination to improve the motive power.[38] Manson went back to being works manager and remained as such until 1882.

For his first engines on the SER, James intended to develop the 0-4-2 freight type, of which he had built a good many in Scotland. Apparently there was local objection to this and instead he got out a 5 foot, 1 inch 0-6-0, designated Class o. With 18 inch × 26 inch cylinders, 1,034 sq. ft heating surface, 140 lbs boiler pressure and 15.25 sq. ft grates, they were typical Stirling family products with the Ramsbottom valves mounted on the third boiler ring, immediately ahead of the firebox. Twelve were built in 1878/9 but unfortunately they were not entirely successful; poor steaming, priming from the boiler and hot boxes in the rear coupled wheels were perennial problems. Consequently, later versions had boilers with reduced tube space and alterations to the fireboxes and grates as well as other modifications. This seemed to do the trick because between 1882 and 1899 a further 102 were put into traffic. Wainwright later fitted domed boilers and his own form of cab, these rebuilds being known as o1.[39] Of this class, BR No. 31065 survived being dumped; it was dismantled in a field for several years before being preserved on the Bluebell Railway, where it can still be seen.

Though it is probably unfair to do so, a locomotive engineer is usually judged on the performance of his express engines. Certainly that is the case with Patrick Stirling, and James's appointment to Ashford had at its heart improving that aspect of the railway's work. His 'A' class 4-4-0s (1879–81) were clearly smaller wheeled versions of the G&SW class, though without the spread fan openings in the splashers, albeit with a form of the skirting plates attached to the running boards. The driving wheel diameter was 6 foot, ½ inch, which raises obvious questions. Research in the twentieth century showed that differences of a couple of inches in driving wheel diameter made no difference to performance. While an express engine would benefit from large wheels, there was nothing to choose between, say, 6 feet, 2 inches and 6 feet, 9 inches. So the 1 inch and sometimes 0.5 inch differences to be found not just on Stirling engines can be seen, in hindsight, to have been pointless. The A class were not outstandingly successful but handled adequately the heavy seaside fast trains to Ramsgate and the semi-fast trains on the difficult Tonbridge–Hastings line.[40]

Two years after the A class came out, the need became apparent for larger locomotives to work the Kent coast boat trains and this led to the well-known F class, the first appearing in 1883. These have some claim to be regarded as James's best engines. To pause for a moment on trifles, the usual Stirling appearance was considerably improved, with the cab front combining in a graceful curve with the rear splasher; the skirt plates became a conventional valence below the running board. A coupling rod box finished the job. The boiler was the usual domeless type with the valves mounted on the third ring, a most inelegant arrangement that could have been easily improved by fitting even a painted-over bonnet. Most noticeably, the driving wheels were increased to 7 foot diameter, as with the G&SW 4-4-0s. Beyond that, this class was much larger with 18 inch (later 19 inches) × 26 inch cylinders; 1,020 sq. ft heating surface; 150, later 160 lbs boiler pressure; and a 16.75 sq. ft grate. The boilers steamed well but were prone to priming, due possibly to differences in the chemical content of the water in south-eastern England as compared with eastern England and Scotland, where the Stirlings experienced less of this problem. No. 240, named *Onward*, was exhibited at the 1889 Paris Exhibition and later ran on the PLM with LBSCR 0-4-2 *Edward Blount*, on some runs without coupling rods.[41] Running against the PLM's own 4-4-0s and the rebuilt Crampton No. 604, No. 240 performed well both in terms of speed and coal consumption.[42]

The SER tended, for a long time, to be something of a joke. *The Times* thundered that the Kentish companies should not even bother to improve their services for they could never aspire to the repute of such as the Great Northern. And Hamilton Ellis, referring to James Stirling's engines as being 'much too good for the majority of the trains they had to run', went on to say about its carriages:

> … the thirds were shocking things, ancient, pokey and fly blown… they were quite good by the standards of the early 60s. … By the 90s they had come down in the world, but were travelling further afield, taking the fruit picker to Paddock Wood, the hopper to Headcorn, the Sunday school to Hastings and Bill and his girl to Folkestone for the day.[43]

Lack of investment in new rolling stock was just one result of the ridiculous warfare that the SER pursued with the Chatham, nearly bankrupting both companies. That said, Acworth makes it clear that the reality, on the important services, was much different: 'there is little of which passengers can complain in the Continental services' and: 'One morning I saw quite accidentally a table of the workings of all the up trains into London Bridge between 8 and 11 am on the previous five days... no train had been more 6 minutes late, very few were more than 2 or 3, while the great majority were up to time.'[44]

Going back to the comment by Hamilton Ellis, it is interesting to compare the F class with Patrick's 8 footers. For the 1895 Race to the North the GNR again used the Stirling singles, both 2-2-2s and the 8 footers, though not from the last batch, which were generally bigger, but the 1884 series. No. 775, which turned in the best run in 1895, at that time retained 18 inch cylinders with 160 lbs pressure. As a comparison the tractive effort of No. 775 was 12,650 lbs and that of the F class, as then running, 15,200 lbs. The track power potential of the F class with coupled wheels was therefore clearly superior to the 4-2-2. No. 775's best run in the 1895 Race was when it hauled the 8 p.m. from King's Cross, which ran from the stop at Grantham to York, 82.7 miles, in 76 minutes; the maximum speed was 73.5 at Newark and remained above 62 for the next 50 miles to Selby.[45] A good run certainly but, as Nock comments generally, although the 'Stirling engines put up good, solid, reliable work... it was perhaps the least sensational of any'. Given Stirling's attitude to speed mentioned earlier, one should not, despite everything, be too surprised by that.

In fact, speeds in the upper 70s and as high as 86 mph were recorded, usually with light loads in the region of down gradients.[46] In the 1880s GNR expresses, powered by Stirling singles, were said to be the fastest in the world and there would be little incentive to do more than keep to booked time: what was the point of doing even better than was already the best! It may also have been officially discouraged, lest it become the expected. With the kind of load already indicated, and with careful handling, it might just have been possible to push an 8-footer to 90 mph.[47] In addition to the speeds that are well authenticated, there are the exploits of certain of these engines in getting up out of King's Cross to Holloway in 3½ minutes and sometimes less. Given that the exit from this terminus was known to tax the Gresley A1 Pacifics, this was no mean achievement. For all that, I have to stick my neck out by saying that James Stirling's F class would have done better, giving the GNR a more sensational start than his brother's engines provided. This is the kind of consideration that enthusiasts for the Stirling singles tend to ignore; good though they were, and I admit, to look at too, by the 1890s something rather more advanced ought to have been on the drawing board.

1885 was a notable year in the Stirling family for good and bad reasons. In the first place Patrick's son, Mathew, was appointed Locomotive Superintendent of the Hull & Barnsley Railway from May 1885, taking over from the interim consulting engineer, William Kirtley of Chatham fame. This was what the Americans would call a 'short line', with a main route from Hull to Cudworth, where it joined the Midland, totalling 53 miles, and with branches adding a further 13 miles to the total; there were some difficult grades on the line, making operation of loose-coupled coal trains very difficult. It was built because of local discontent with the activities of the monopoly North Eastern, about which the details as set out by Ahrons take some beating for their sheer delightfulness.[48] Sufficient here to record that Mathew remained the only Locomotive Superintendent of this concern, in office until the Hull & Barnsley was absorbed by its deadliest rival, and then became part of the LNER. On so short a railway there was no call for a large stock of motive power. On taking over, he found that there were forty-two locomotives to Kirtley's design running and left them to it until 1889 apart from ordering three Kitson-designed 0-4-0WT shunting engines, delivered in 1886–9. Though a saddle tank, the ex-Cardiff Railway locomotive GWR 1338 now preserved at Didcot is not dissimilar, with the same Kitson valve gear above the footplate.

The other incident in 1885 was of a rather different nature: an attempt on the life of James Stirling. We lack the space here to recount this in full but it can be found in *Back Track* magazine.[49] The nub of the matter was that an alarm on a stationary boiler in Ashford works had been rigged to stop it going off and the water level had dropped to a dangerous level. This got back to Stirling, who decided that the boiler needed watching both at night and during the day and ordered the day man to take the night watch. This worthy protested the order without apparently stating the reason for his so doing, but Stirling was adamant. A day or two later the workman purchased a revolver and attempted to shoot Stirling with it. Enquiry revealed that the man, who had a lifetime of misfortune behind him, was consumed with anxiety about losing pay as a result of the change to his working conditions. Attempting to kill Stirling was a stupid reaction to the problem but it underlines the fact that even well-intentioned executives, unaware of the full facts of a case, can unintentionally make decisions that threaten their employees' well-being. Stirling was badly shaken by the incident and so would anyone. But to paraphrase someone else, he ought to have been told, he ought to have asked, most of all, he ought to have known what was involved in the order he had given.

Mathew's first engines for the H&B were some 0-6-0 freight engines, followed three years later by 0-6-0Ts and then five 0-6-2 passenger tanks originally intended for the Lancashire, Derbyshire & East Coast Railway but purchased by the H&B to became class F1. They were the largest tank locomotives the H&B ever owned and contrasted greatly with the standard Stirlings then in service and built thereafter, for they had domed boilers. Mathew continued the straight back boiler tradition of his family, even with the massive 1907 Class A 0-8-0s built to take 780-ton trains from Cudworth to Hull and return with trainloads of sixty-five vehicles, a turn normally requiring double heading. Basically they were enlarged 0-6-0s with smaller wheels and 19 inch × 26 inch cylinders. It is their boilers that are the most interesting part of the design. 14 feet, 6 inches long and 5 feet, 6 inches in diameter, with 1,859 sq. ft heating surface, pressed originally to 200 lbs, the Stirling straight back boiler was merged with a Belpaire firebox having a grate area of 22 sq. ft. This is the only example of the use of this firebox by either of the three Stirlings and may have been a suggestion of the manufacturer's, the Yorkshire Engine Company, keenness to overcome the limits of the Stirling domeless boiler. They were certainly not easy machines to crew; H&B footplatemen, who called them 'Tinies', were paid *6d* a day extra for the experience. As with other H&B locomotives, as soon as the NER had taken them into stock they put in hand a programme of reboilering them with domed boilers. It must say something about the originals that the last 0-8-0s was not converted until 1928. The prolific numbers of GNR and NER freight engines of various 0-8-0 and 2-8-0 classes, together with ROD 04 locomotives, meant that the fifteen H&B engines became redundant soon after these conversions had been carried out. After being withdrawn in 1931, the boilers were used again as rebuilds on the NER Q5/2 0-8-0s, of which the last was not withdrawn until 1949.

Kirtley's 2-4-0s, ordered for the H&B before Mathew's appointment as Locomotive Superintendent, handled the passenger trains between Hull and Cudworth, working forward with the through trains to Sheffield, and were replaced from 1910 by five 4-4-0s, class J, designed by Mathew Stirling and built by Kitson's. They remained on these trains even after the H&B station in Hull was closed and passenger services transferred to the NER Paragon terminus. Like most of the other Stirling engines, their original domeless boilers were replaced by a NER domed boiler from 1929. From about 1932 they took turns with NER locomotives on services to Doncaster, York, Leeds and Scarborough. Despite this, little work was found for them; they spent a good deal of their last days in store. The last was scrapped in September 1934.[50]

The summer of 1889 was difficult for Patrick Stirling; he suffered from some loss of strength and had to recuperate to restore it. Aged sixty-nine, he really ought to have recognised that this was the time to take well-earned retirement but he did not do that. He returned to work and continued in office until 1895, when he announced a less than resolute intention of resigning. The Board took it as being rather more certain and discussed an appointment with H. A. Ivatt. A deal was done shortly before the old man died. Whether James interpreted this as a warning we cannot say. It may be that he saw the way things were moving and decided it was time to go. By 1895 the operators were asking for more powerful engines and very reluctantly Stirling gave them the B class, the F series 4-4-0s with larger boilers. In terms of appearance the most outstanding thing about these locomotives was the discarding of the Stirling cab in favour of a square, more commodious layout. James took the opportunity of the establishment of a co-ordinating committee to administer the operations of the SER and the LCDR as his opportunity to retire, and he went in 1898. He enjoyed nearly twenty years' retirement. Nephew Mathew, Patrick's second son, leaving the H&B in 1922, continued to live in Hull until his death in 1931. This was not the end of the Stirling family, for several generations have continued to be active in engineering.[51]

Chapter 5

The Drummond Brothers

Sixty years ago, Didcot Town Football Club's ground lay about 150 yards south of the main WR railway line and from its terraces, such as they were, it was possible to see everything that passed on the embankment, which in those days meant almost every ex-GWR class locomotive then running. It was usually during the first half of play that the section of seating occupied by Didcot's engine drivers would burst into laughter and robust, even ribald, comment. This would accompany the appearance of the 15.35 departure for Newbury, pausing momentarily for the signal before proceeding onto the branchline that would carry it to Newbury and eventually, some three hours later, through Eastleigh to Southampton Terminus. The object of this hilarity would be the engine hauling the train, an ex-LSWR T9 4-4-0, referred to on one occasion as 'old Bailey on the corporation steamroller'! This was my introduction to the LSWR and particularly to the man who designed the T9s, Dugald Drummond. I did not then know that in the late nineteenth and early twentieth centuries, and indeed for long afterwards, travelling by train from Calisle to Inverness and Thurso either by way of Glasgow or Edinburgh, involving as it did travel over three or even four major railways, did not however involve any particular change in the general appearance of the locomotive at the front of the train. They were Drummond engines, large and small, built over a long period for all four railways, which, with their derivatives, imposed a family resemblance that was only ever achieved by one other railway in any part of the UK.

Dugald Drummond has come down to us with a reputation few other locomotive engineers ever had and certainly would not have aspired to. There is a story, which must come from our old friend Hamilton Ellis[1], that a tradesman called at Dugald's official residence to enquire about redecorating it. The whimpering maid who answered the door did not know what to say but a booming voice from within declared, 'Tar the bluidy place all over'! It is said that fellow Scot John McIntosh was the only man from whom he would take banter and this is very much the accepted view of him: an ill-tempered and bully boy Scotsman given to outbursts of invective that, heard third-hand, are amusing, though not so if you were on the receiving end of them. In an age when discipline was more than severe, such behaviour, to have warranted notice, suggests that Dugald Drummond was indeed a monster. The late Eric Forge[2] testified to this conclusion but relates an incident that tells a different story. Having severely berated a driver for going past a signal and having heard that the man was worried about his wife who was unwell and, with four children to look after, badly in need of a rest, he admonished the fellow with the words: 'Well, I'll no say any more aboot it this time, but see you don't come before me agen, keep your mind on your job in future!' As he was turning to go, Drummond called him back. 'Tak this,' he said, 'and get her a bottle.' 'This' was a sovereign (£1), which would have bought many bottles of whatever medicinal product she could ever have needed.

No one is born with such a personality and there must have been something in his background that caused his manner to be so tyrannical. He was born at Ardrossan, Ayrshire, on 1 January 1840, eldest son of the permanent way inspector of the Bowling district of the North British Railway. His younger brother, Peter, was born 13 August 1850, by which time their father had moved to Polmont.[3] Both did their apprenticeships with Forrest & Barr in Glasgow. The elder Drummond was for a time attached to Stroudley, working with him at Cowlairs (NBR). Peter followed his brother around until the elder went off to head a new private manufacturing enterprise, when he joined the Highland Railway as Locomotive Superintendent. Peter is sometimes spoken of as the 'nicer' of the Drummond brothers but, for myself, I think that Dugald's behaviour was the result of tragedy, undeserved claims of dishonesty and, on the LSWR, his single-minded determination to root out drunkenness, all of which was pervaded with his genuine comprehension of the realities of the industrial scene as it was at the latter end of the nineteenth century. Some men who reach the top 'spit on their past', as it has been termed, but, despite the insults later to be aimed at him, Drummond did not do this. Hamilton Ellis wrote, '…he would countenance no victimization; he summarily dismissed one of his senior officers for improper severity. Nor would he have anything to do with coercion of his men in labour disputes. He was strongly interested in the welfare and education of his men…'[4] Drinking while in charge of a working locomotive was and should be a serious offence. I believe that I have seen an example of this myself, as recently as the 1970s, and it was certainly a serious problem 120 years ago; I just wonder if a more enlightened view of its triggers would have served better the cause of eradicating it.

Dugald married Jane Young on 2 June 1865 and immediately took his new wife to Inverness, where he had been appointed foreman erector in the Lochgorm Workshops of the Highland Railway by his mentor, William Stroudley. Their joint departure from Cowlairs had been precipitated by a row with the then Works Manager, Samuel Johnson.[5] The Drummonds had four sons and four daughters; the first son, born in August 1866, died within a month; the second, born in 1867, died about twelve months later, after the birth of a third, Walter, who survived into his thirties. It is suggested that the deaths of the first two sons badly affected Drummond, and in both cases the cause is likely to have been the insanitary conditions in which they lived. By the time that Walter was born, the Drummonds had moved to a new address, consequent on his becoming Works Manager, and this may well have been what saved him from similar illnesses. The reader might well wonder about the general level of housing sanitation in Inverness at this time; given that a senior artisan of an important railway company could only afford to house his family in such conditions, one has to wonder what it was like for the ordinary railway labourer. Neither Stroudley nor Drummond, particularly the latter, were popular with David Jones, whose official position was equivalent to Drummond's though he considered himself the senior. Mrs Jones is alleged to have claimed that the Drummonds were not 'socially acceptable', an observation that Drummond would not have appreciated.[6] Pure snobbery I think, the disdain that an Englishman (the Joneses were from Manchester) might feel for a Scot little above the manual class and possessed of a virulent tongue; we might conjecture also that Mrs Jones had experience thereof.

There is also another possible cause, or at least encouragement, of Dugald Drummond's irascible behaviour and that may be associated with the Tay Bridge disaster. In 1869 Stroudley left the Highland to go south to Brighton and Dugald followed him the following year, becoming his assistant.[7] In 1875 Drummond broke out on his own, going on invitation to the North British as Locomotive Superintendent in succession to Wheatley.[8] This brought him back to Cowlairs but Johnson had gone to the Midland two years previously. He was, therefore, in post at the time of the Tay Bridge disaster. A locomotive of his design was normally rostered to the afternoon train from Edinburgh to Dundee but the failure of 0-4-2T *Ladybank* meant that Wheatley 4-4-0 No. 224 took on that task. Because of this, it was considered that he was free to speak as an expert witness at the enquiry. Sir Thomas Bouch, architect of the bridge, claimed that the rear portion of the train had been blown off the rails and fouled the high girders, bringing them down.[9] Whether this was a deliberate attempt to pass the buck we cannot know, but Drummond was able to show, by reference to marks on the lines and the condition of the axles, that the train had fallen vertically when the high girders collapsed. Bouch was the scapegoat for what happened, and indeed probably deserved to be, but the NBR could not have felt enamoured of its own officer testifying against the man they had employed to build the bridge. Within two years he was gone; Middlemass says that '... it is known now ... that at that time an investigation was also being considered into yet another unexplained financial discrepancy in Cowlairs accounts...'[10] The NBR Board had got rid of Wheatley in similar fashion and this may have been just another ruse to free itself of a man prepared to speak an unfortunate truth. Drummond was an honest man (I think we can assume that) and this kind of allegation, for all its falsehood, would have been an irritant constantly in the back of his mind. On the basis of all these facts, it is no wonder that his was a very difficult personality.

We should note that Peter Drummond, finishing his apprenticeship in 1871, followed his brother to the Brighton, where he remained until 1876 when he re-joined Dugald at Cowlairs as under manager, a position not recognised by the Board but which was doubtless useful experience.[11] Another useful purpose may have been that it enabled him to marry Mary McKay Phillips on 26 August 1876. They eventually had three daughters. Again, when Dugald moved on to the Caledonian in 1882, Peter followed him as Works Manager at St Rollox and Assistant Locomotive Superintendent. It was only when the elder Drummond became involved in an Australian engineering project that Peter took off on his own as Locomotive Superintendent of the Highland, succeeding, be it noted, the David Jones whose wife had been so contemptuous of his brother.

Before moving on, a word here, out of strict chronology, about the Australasian Locomotive Engine Works Co. (ALEWC) would not be inappropriate. Only the sketchiest details of this project were known before J. E. Chacksfield investigated the matter in depth; readers wanting to read chapter and verse are referred to his book on the Drummonds.[12] It is sufficient here to repeat that an Australian engineering entrepreneur with the name of Henry Hudson, finding some interest in the New South Wales government in promoting a locomotive manufacturing company, came to the UK to seek capital.[13] There were a great many Scots, particularly Glaswegians, engaged in engineering in Australia and, going north, he offered Dugald the position of Managing Director of the new company. Drummond accordingly resigned from the Caledonian and sailed for Sydney, where he found matters very different to what he had been led to believe. Reading between the lines, it is possible to conclude that Drummond found his area of control was severely restricted by what we would call 'red tape'. Ever the autocrat, this would not have appealed to him at all. Moreover, orders for locomotives were not forthcoming. Unsurprisingly, he resigned his position and returned to the UK. The company that he left behind became Clyde Engineering and eventually an important builder of rolling stock for Australian railways. Some authors suggest that Drummond's influence can be seen in subsequent NSWGR locomotives but I am not wholly convinced. It was certainly not as obvious as Swindon design is in Lucy's NN class 4-6-0, almost a copy of the Churchward Saint. Back in the UK Drummond set up as a locomotive builder, trading as D. Drummond & Co. After 1895, when he became Locomotive Superintendent of the LSWR, it was run by his sons George and Walter as the Glasgow Railway Engineering Company and survived to be taken over by Beardmore's in the 1930s.[14]

Going back to 1875, Dugald Drummond's first locomotive designs showed the Stroudley influence strongly; it is particularly marked in the 2-2-2s Nos 474 *Glasgow* and 475 *Berwick*, completed in 1876, and which were almost exact copies of Stroudley's 1874 2-2-2s for the Brighton. Cylinders at 17 inches × 24 inches were identical and the diameter of the boiler and heating surface were virtually identical. Stroudley did not like 'opening' the barrel core and therefore combined the dome and safety valve, which Drummond also copied, though with the Ramsbottom valve rather than the spring balance type, a design feature that he retained for all his locomotives except the LSWR 4-6-0s. Drummond used larger driving wheels with a consequent increase in axle weight but this was minimal. The Stroudley cab and tender were also duplicated, completing what to all intents and purposes was a replica of the Brighton engine. Ahrons records that they were usually to be found working the morning expresses from Glasgow to

Edinburgh, returning with the evening trains that carried through coaches from King's Cross. The booked time in 1876 was 70 minutes, including the contretemps involved in scaling the 1:41 to 1:50 Cowlairs incline on which assistance was provided by stationery engine wire haulage.[15] For freight work and local passenger services, Drummond constructed only 0-6-0s and 0-4-4Ts.

Whether it is fair to ascribe to Drummond's design Caledonian 4-2-2 No. 123 I am never too sure. The machine that currently stands in the Glasgow Transport Museum is certainly not what it is claimed to be. The original locomotive was built, together with a 4-4-0, by Neilson's in 1886 for display at the Edinburgh International Exhibition of that year, where it won a gold medal. The detail design work was almost certainly done by the Chief Draughtsmen at St Rollox and of Neilson & Co. working together. It would have been advantageous to Neilson's to demonstrate the inclination of the Caledonian to order its engines from them, so turning it out in full Caledonian fig is understandable. The Drummond piston and blastpipe design as used on his Class 60 was used again, in addition to the combined dome and safety valve boiler, though the chimney was different. In normal service it ran with a standard Caledonian tender. In 1905 No. 123 was rebuilt with a Caledonian 0-6-0 boiler, and then again in 1924, running in LMS Crimson Lake livery numbered 14010. It was withdrawn from service in 1935. Although clearly not then in Caledonian condition, it was repainted in that railway's blue livery and kept at St Rollox works until 1958. Then, probably in response to the Western Region's successful operation of *City of Truro*, No. 123 was restored, with another replacement boiler, for work hauling special trains. It is with this boiler still in place that No. 123 now rests in Glasgow, resplendent in the completely unhistorical Caledonian blue! What is being celebrated is not the historical reality of the engine but its time running special trains in the late 1950s/early 60s.

Its real importance lies in its use on the Carlisle–Edinburgh section of the West Coast route to Edinburgh in the 1888 Race to the North. It is not necessary to go into too much detail about this; the literature on both the 1888 and 1895 'races' are legion.[16] It is sufficient here to note that the challenge was to get from London to Edinburgh first, the Great Northern and North Eastern by what might be supposed the more direct route up the east coast, and the LNWR and Caledonian over the west coast. The total mileages by each route were 399.7 for the west coast and 393.2 for the east.

The gradients on the west side were much harder, with Shap, Beattock and Cobbinshaw in the 'down' direction out of proportion to anything on the east side. The Caledonian had to combat the worst of these: Beattock and Cobbinshaw, which were 1:75 and 1:100–120 at their worst. The gradients were somewhat easier going south but climbing them from the other side still made severe demands on motive power. What is so extraordinary, certainly at first sight, is that on these severe gradients the Caledonian used the Neilson/Drummond 4-2-2 No. 123!

Locomotives with single driving axles went out of favour in the late 1860s and early 1870s. The increasing weights of trains were becoming too much for the low adhesion weight of the single wheeler on starting, accelerating and on gradients, particularly in inclement weather. Sanding became very important but when it was most needed, in wet conditions, the humidity in the air would reduce its fluidity and seriously reduce its usefulness. The American practice of putting a sand dome on top of the boiler was not always an answer to this problem. Only the GWR and the GNR, among important railways, persisted with single wheelers during this period, principally because their main lines were relatively easy, but also because Patrick Stirling in particular believed coupled wheels offered no advantage. In his favour, Ahrons cites evidence of deficiencies in iron and in wheel balancing that undermined the apparently obvious superiority of using two driving axles, either 2-4-0 or 4-4-0.[17] Holt's steam sanding gear, invented in 1886 and first deployed by Johnson on his Spinners the following year, set off a new enthusiasm for single wheelers but No. 123 was not equipped therewith.

I shall discuss Drummond's 4-4-0s in more detail later in this chapter. Before continuing, however, we should note that the dimensions of the 60 or Carbrook class differed little from that of the 4-2-2; the cylinders of both were 18 inches × 26 inches, while the boiler on the single wheeler was slightly smaller with a smaller grate, though the larger driving wheels reduced the tractive effort by about 200 lbs. The adhesion factor was low, well below the ideal of 4.3, strongly suggesting that in theory the use of the 4-4-0 would have been the better policy. Another issue is the well-known propensity of locomotives to 'sit down' on starting and on gradients, a weight transfer to the rear axle that, however slight, with uncompensated trailing wheels detracts from the effective utilisation of the tractive effort. A most important point to note is that the trains that the Caledonian took over from the LNWR at Carlisle were hardly of great tonnage. Four bogies of about 80 tons, not that much more than engine and tender fully laden, was the daily load; anything much greater would have shown the advantage of coupled wheels. The 100.6 miles from Carlisle to Princes Street Station was booked at 112 minutes but No. 123 always arrived early, as much as seconds short of ten minutes before time on 9 August.

As already noted, when Dugald Drummond went off to Australia his brother Peter was appointed, from more than thirty applicants, Locomotive Superintendent of the Highland. His predecessor, David Jones, is celebrated as the designer of the first British 4-6-0, delivered in 1894; the class was generally known as Jones Goods although they were used on passenger trains from their first few months at work. Drummond now committed the almost clichéd sin among locomotive engineers of casting to the four winds the works of his predecessor – very nearly. The Highland Railway, which ran up the spine of Scotland from Perth to Inverness and further north, was, inevitably, an undulating line that reached the highest point on a British railway at Druimuachdar Summit, 1,484 feet above sea level. In 1898 a new Inverness direct line was opened from Aviemore that gave a shorter but more difficult run; in particular, northwards from Aviemore there was the 12-mile climb at 1:60 to Slochd Summit, 1,315 feet. The completion of this line meant a demand for more powerful engines and it is known that a design for a 4-6-0 passenger engine with outside cylinders and 5 foot, 9 inch driving wheels, developed from the 1894 Big Goods, was actually on the drawing board when an accident forced David Jones to resign. Drummond did not proceed with this design, it is suggested, because of a need for economy.[18] Instead he turned out 4-4-0s, known, if you are a Scot, as the Wee Bens. These were typical of the Drummond family output, with inside cylinders, boiler with combined dome and safety valve and robustly built.

The Jones Loch class worked the best trains between Perth and Inverness and there was no significant change to this arrangement after the Small Bens were introduced. These were slightly smaller than the Loch class, which had 19 inch × 24 inch cylinders with piston valves and, despite larger driving wheels, about the same tractive effort. Arguably they were under-boilered, a factor in sixteen being rebuilt around 1927 with Caledonian Jumbo 0-6-0 boilers designed, ironically enough, by Peter's brother. New cylinders and in some cases new frames were also fitted at the same time. Most of the Lochs were also rebuilt with similar boilers.[19] The contretemps over the preservation of *Ben Alder* needs no repeating here. My question is what justified its preservation in the first place; while they gave good service throughout their lives, it was not spectacular. It cannot surely have been this eulogy, published after it was withdrawn:

> Believe it or not, the Ben, in her stately progress with two carriages told me plainly that Drummond and his ilk had put something into their 'bairns' which the moderns will never experience. For me it was a really nostalgic moment to feel the motion of that engine beneath my feet. There was a gentleness, a flowing unity of co-ordinated movement which the 'big 'uns' will never achieve. There wasn't a harsh sound; in fact, apart from the soft, rounded clink of the coupling rods against the driving pin washers, *Ben Alder* wound her way over the flat uninteresting stretch almost noiselessly.[20]

During the period from 1899 onwards Drummond schemed out a number of refinements of the Small Ben that never got beyond the drawing board.[21] Much the most interesting was the 1901 scheme for a 6 foot, 6 inch locomotive with a much enlarged boiler, having a 27 sq. ft grate, 1,660 sq. ft heating surface and 19 inch × 26 inch cylinders. This also shows the incorporation of Dugald's cross water tubes in the firebox, adding 215 sq. ft to the heating surface. While the Highland's poor financial performance was also a factor, it seems likely that probable restrictions on its sphere of operation was the main reason why this proposal was not developed. When a new 4-4-0 type was built, the Large Ben, the locomotives were not significantly bigger than their predecessors except in the boiler. Fatally, the firebox was no bigger than on the Small Ben and consequently they showed no improvement on the performance of the 'smaller' variety. Their effectiveness is certainly questioned by the construction, in 1917, of three further Jones Loch class 4-4-0s. The Large Bens were later rebuilt with feed water heaters and superheaters but the cost of these alterations probably outweighed any benefit they provided.

While the second batch of Small Bens was being delivered from Lochgorm, a 4-6-0 passenger type was at last delivered from Dubbs in 1900. These were very significant engines and I will discuss them further down. In 1912 Peter Drummond accepted an offer to become Locomotive, Carriage and Wagon Superintendent of the Glasgow & South Western Railway at Kilmarnock,[22] where he was responsible for two further 4-4-0 designs, the

131 and 137 classes, outshopped in 1913 and 1915. The 131 class, said to be a direct derivation from the LSWR D15 class,[23] was described as needing 'careful handling ... to get the best out of [them]. Uphill they were sluggish and they rolled badly so that endeavors to regain lost time were not recommended particularly on the sinuous roads in the Paisley and Glasgow area.'[24]. In the 137 class superheating was tried, with apparent success, until drivers' prejudices were allowed to go uncontested. Consequently the 137 class lasted but a short time on first class work.

In 1895, after his Australian contretemps and disappointing business experience, Dugald Drummond returned to office as a salaried locomotive engineer on the London & South Western Railway. This was a long way from Scotland and the reader is permitted to consider its meaning. He was, of course, no stranger to the south of England, having spent six years at Brighton with Stroudley, but it would be useful to know just what initiated his going there. His fifteen years at the head of South Western locomotive affairs were, to state the least, interesting, marked as they were with success and abject failure. He is best known for his 4-4-0s, of which there were six varieties in two general operational roles. The best known were the T9s with which I opened this chapter. There is no doubt that in their original condition they did first class work, giving their designer a reputation that, overall, he does not really deserve.

It makes sense to consider all the 4-4-0s built by the Drummond brothers together rather than as isolated classes of engine. The 4-4-0 is often spoken of as being the 'typical American' locomotive, although it gave way, relatively soon, to the 2-6-0, 2-8-0 and leading bogie types. If Britain has any such typical locomotive then to my mind the 4-6-0 fits that description. However, there were many classes of inside cylinder, inside frame 4-4-0 built in Britain; the first, by Wheatley for the NBR in 1871, included the unfortunate engine that went down with the Tay Bridge. The last such was the SR L1 class, completed in 1926. Mention should also be made of the last outside cylinder examples: the LNER D49 (1927), the SR Schools (1930) and the Irish Great Northern 4-4-0s, originally built in 1932 and rebuilt as late as 1947–50.

Dugald Drummond's first locomotives of this wheel type were built for the North British Railway in 1876; the last recognisably of his design, the D15 class, were built for the LSWR in 1912. The appearance of a Drummond locomotive will be well known, even to young people in the twenty-first century. Two preserved M7 0-4-4Ts have the original boiler layout and, even though T9 30120 has an extended smokebox and stove pipe chimney, the Drummond form can be seen clearly. More important are the elements that remained constant almost throughout every design: inside cylinders with steam chest between and valves driven by Stephenson valve gear with four eccentrics. The firebox was placed between the driving wheels and, from the T9s on, was provided with cross water tubes, mounted in two groups with access through manholes in the sides of the firebox casing, providing extra heating surface and improved water circulation.[25] The restriction that resulted from dropping the firebox between the driving wheels led to an extraordinary departure from common practice, to be described later. Peter followed his brother's general theme through much of his own work; his last 4-4-0s, as we have seen, were constructed in 1915 and therefore the broad swathe of Drummond 4-4-0 design lasted from 1876 to 1915. The diagram on page 17 of the central image section shows most of the dimensions of all the types that come under that heading.

The most obvious reaction to this table is to note that over a period of not quite forty years, development in terms of size and power was modest. Tractive effort is not a description of power but, if we accept it as one indication of a locomotive's potential performance, then the outstanding point is that during that forty years, it increased 73 per cent overall. However, the D15 was a significantly bigger engine than those that had gone before. The tractive effort of the Highland Large Ben was only 40 per cent greater than Dugald's first 4-4-0s. In a paper to the Institution of Civil Engineers,[26] Dugald stated that encouraged by him to drive on a low cut off and full regulator, his 66 4-4-0s showed an ihp of 940 at 51 mph, and 856 ihp on Beattock with a full regulator and cut off between 33 and 37 per cent.[27] These are the only reliable indicator diagrams we have for Drummond's 4-4-0s and bearing in mind that identical boiler and cylinder dimensions will produce wildly different tractive effort figures if they are mounted on differently sized driving wheels, any overall review of the developmental process of these designs must fall back on their component dimensions. Thus an assessment of boiler dimensions shows that overall the heating surface in Drummond boilers increased by 57 per cent; excluding the D15, the figure comes down to 41 per cent. Increased heating surface was generally due to increased lengths of firebox, enlarged from 6 feet, 4 inches in the C8 to 8 feet, 4 inches in the D15. Boiler diameters changed only latterly; not until the S11 class came out did a 5 foot diameter boiler appear. The Large Ben had 5 foot, 3 inch diameter boilers, in reality to very little effect. Piston valves were first used by Jones in the Loch class but neither Drummond used them until Dugald incorporated them in his 4-6-0s.

The second Race to the North lit up the night skies for a few weeks in 1895, when the 'finishing line' was Aberdeen rather than Edinburgh. This meant that, instead of continuing towards Edinburgh, Caledonian trains took the Glasgow line at Strawfrank Junction to run through Carstairs, and then turned north-east at Motherwell, avoiding Glasgow. Ignoring for now that Drummond-derived locomotives were used by both the North British on the east coast line[28] and the Caledonian, the best performance by one of his own engines was probably that of 4-4-0 No. 90.[29] No. 90 took three vehicles from Carlisle to Perth, 150.8 miles, in 149.5 minutes, an overall average just better than even time. The load was very light: 72.5 tons. The 10 miles from Beattock station to the summit were covered in 13.5 minutes, a pass-to-pass average of 44.4 mph; the speed at Beattock station had been 66.8 mph, with that at the summit of 53 mph. This compares with 4-2-2 No. 123, which, on its best run, reached the summit of Beattock in almost the same time but from a pass speed of 60 mph had come down to 36.5 at the summit. Viewed overall, especially by a passenger on the train merely going from one place to another, the performance of both was very similar, though Nock reports that the 4-4-0 was held back in the early stages of the run. Nock also gives details of Nos 78 and 90 double-heading a train of 207 tons' tare, which reached the summit of Beattock in 14 minutes, 34 seconds, passing the station at about 65 mph and stopping to detach the banker at the summit. This is more than double the weight of the train logged on the 'race special' and, even allowing that it was banked, to have reached the top of the incline, with a requirement to stop, in no more than about one minute extra is not a trivial achievement.[30] On the LSWR, Dugald's T9s gave some spirited performances, especially on the Ocean Mail traffic. Despite that, their best work was done after Urie and later Maunsell had removed the cross water tubes and superheated the boilers.

In Scotland the legacy left by Dugald Drummond was long-lasting, even ignoring any contribution to the family reputation that was made by Peter. Mathew Holmes was Drummond's successor on the North British Railway and his 574, 633, 729, 592 and West Highland classes, particularly the early types, were clearly derived from Drummond except in one important respect. Inexplicably, he replaced the Drummond/Stroudley cab with one clearly based on the Stirling family's shelter. More 'manly' it might have been but on a wet, windy night anywhere north of Carlisle it must have been an actual hindrance to the ability of the driver to keep a good lookout. Holmes's successor in 1903, W. P. Reid, rebuilt some of his predecessor's engines and turned out his own, much bigger 4-4-0s. The Stirling cab was discarded at once but the Drummond type did not reappear, Reid introducing a rather angular thing with one side window immediately adjacent to the cab front. Even so, the general run of the engine still owed much to Drummond. Back on the Caledonian, Lambie continued his predecessor's general approach, as did McIntosh. The Dunalaister IV 4-4-0s showed their lineage as clearly as a T9 or D15.

The demands made on locomotives by the Scottish railway lines were rather different from those of the LSWR. Gradients on the LSWR were not always easy but they held nothing to the demands of the long climbs and circuitous routes of the Caledonian, Highland and North British. Furthermore, the frequency of trains in Scotland was much less than in southern England; such railways also lacked easy access to investment, nor did they always get a very good return on it. Middlemass put it somewhat one-sidedly, but was nevertheless to the point when he wrote,

> It has become quite commonplace for contemporary railway authors to deride Scottish steam locomotive development as lamentably failing to reach beyond the late Victorian era. G. J. Churchward is often quoted by contemporaries, but such facile near-dismissal of the Drummond's and the McIntosh's of this world calmly glosses over the fact that the mighty Great Western functioned in the richest areas of the UK and that all through history, the Scottish economy has, for a variety of reasons lagged far behind that of its infinitely more prosperous southern neighbour.[31]

It is hard not to agree with this; at the same time it is important to note that a number of significant developments in design originated in Scotland. The trend towards larger boilers has been ascribed to McIntosh and the Dunalastair classes, to which I would add that, for me, the Jones Goods was the real precursor for the future.

With six axles, outside cylinders and a practical layout, the Big Goods not only made the engineering leap from the traditional 4-4-0 but laid the foundations of the British locomotive of the future. Previously Jones had used the straight link motion and double frame layout associated with Alexander Allan on all his 4-4-0s; even the Strath class, turned out in 1892, had a certain archaic appearance. Discarding the Allan framing while retaining his valve gear gave the Big Goods a state of the art appearance that was later replicated in the Loch 4-4-0s. The dimensions of the 4-6-0s showed a significant advance on previous Scottish practice. With cylinders 20 inches in diameter, a 1,675 sq. ft heating surface, a grate area of 22.6 sq. ft, and 170 lbs pressure, the engine weight was 56 tons. The 5 foot, 3 inch driving wheels gave a tractive effort of 24,500 lbs. These were big engines indeed and it is to their designer's credit that, apart from trifling things like the replacement of the louvred chimney, they remained essentially unaltered throughout their working lives.

There seems little doubt that Peter Drummond was not equal to the abilities of his brother and probably lacked the sparkle of the real executive locomotive engineer. On the GSWR, in addition to his 4-4-0s, he got out both 0-6-0 and 2-6-0 goods engines, both types with inside cylinders of course, and the latter, to casual examination, appearing to be nothing more than the 0-6-0 with a pony truck. This critique of Peter is at least in part suggested by the business of the Castle 4-6-0. I am not entirely certain that it was for reasons of economy that the Jones passenger 4-6-0 was not built, though it certainly is true that the Highland went through several periods when the cash flow was difficult. From a viewpoint of logic it seems more likely that Peter Drummond thought he could do better and shelved the design. Had his Small and Large Bens been as successful as the increasing weight of trains demanded, more of those classes would have been built and possibly developed into a 4-6-0. An inside cylinder 4-6-0 creates difficulties fully evidenced in the overlong boiler on *Cardean* but I don't see that as stopping him. Something better than the Bens was required and *in extremis* he reached for the best quick response to that need; Jones proposed a passenger 4-6-0, suitably got up to look like one of his own engines, with certain design amendments such as the change from piston to slide valves. It was out of character to anything that he had previously built and it is safe to assume, as most observers do, that it originated in the previous Jones proposal.[32]

Driving wheels were 5 feet, 9 inches as opposed to the 6 feet preferred by Drummond; the boilers were larger than those on the Big Goods, with 14 foot, 4½ inch long and 5 foot diameter boilers, 180 lbs pressure and a high heating surface figure at 2,050 sq. ft. The grate area was a commodious 26.5 sq. ft. The nominal figures compare very favourably with the original standard No. 1 boiler developed by Churchward, but that had the advantage of the advanced circulation characteristics of the Belpaire taper boiler and the use of piston valves. The Castles had slide valves and, apart from one experiment, were never superheated. Eventually there were nineteen of them, the last three built as late as 1917 with larger driving wheels and a bigger boiler. That the Castles were a successful design cannot be ignored. They worked the best trains between Inverness and Perth for many years, giving a good account of themselves though double-heading was usually deployed on Druimuachdar, Slochd and Dava summits. Speeds in the 60s were often recorded and 70 mph was attained on occasion.

Most extraordinary of all, there were also fifty built for the French State Railway (L'État) in 1911[33]. They were not the only Drummond lookalikes to work on the Continent: McIntosh engines and developments derived from them ran in Belgium for many years and at least one has been preserved. The French Castles were probably not as well regarded as they were in Scotland, for the État used poor quality coal, requiring a larger firebox. Despite this they continued to work until 1938; three of the class remaining intact at the time of the fall of France, they were put back into service in 1941.[34] The last of the indigenous version was withdrawn and scrapped at Lochgorm works in 1947.

The issue of 4-6-0s is a thorny one in the careers of both Drummonds. That the Castle was a 'Drummondised' version of a Jones design is further substantiated by the outline scheme for a mixed traffic 4-6-0 dated 1907 and signed by his eventual successor, F. G. Smith. This used 5 foot driving wheels and outside cylinders, and was a scaled down version of the Castle. With smaller driving wheels it would have had slightly greater tractive effort than the Castle.[35] It is reasonable to assume that Peter made no contribution to this scheme and it may even have been a job undertaken by Smith without the chief's authorisation. The caveat to the discovery of old drawings is always that an attempt should be made to establish their provenance. One more 4-6-0 proposal is ascribed to Peter, and we will examine that further down.

Unlike some of his contemporaries, Dugald was aware that the provision of larger fireboxes was a requirement that ran hand in hand with greater boiler power. On 4-4-0 locomotives the firebox sat down between the driving wheels and its length determined the driving wheel base and thus the length of the coupling rods. Bearing in mind Ahrons' strictures, already noted, on poor manufacturing processes that could lead to contrasting wear on driving wheel tyres, resulting in coupling rods being sprung off their mountings, Drummond's extraordinary first express loco design for the LSWR is not so incomprehensible as some have suggested. The evidence of No. 123 on the 1888 Race to the North was that single wheelers could, in certain circumstances, mirror the work of 4-4-0s. As further evidence of that, Ahrons mentions that the GWR 2-2-2 No. 9 (later named *Victoria*) could 'pull like a coupled engine'.[36] It must have been results like these that encouraged first Webb and then Drummond to get rid of the coupling rods by building 'double singles', thus allowing for the incorporation of a longer firebox. Therefore a non-compound version of the Webb design, a 4-2-2-0 combining the advantages of the single wheeler with the facility for fitting a longer firebox, appeared to be the means by which to provide the express power needed on the Bournemouth and Salisbury trains. The locomotives thus developed – the original T7, No. 720, later rebuilt with a larger boiler, and the later E10 class – were not very successful. Inevitably, it was the uncoupled driving wheels and the failure of the steam sanding gear, essential with these engines, that was their basic drawback.

Astonishingly, when Drummond came to design 4-6-0s he replicated certain aspects of these double single locomotives. By 1903 trains on the LSWR were becoming heavier, particularly with the corridor stock increasingly used on its west of England services. By 1905 even the 6 foot, 7 inch L12 4-4-0s were being stretched; something more powerful clearly meant going to six coupled axles. In 1903, on a visit to St Rollox, Drummond had been impressed by the McIntosh Cardean 4-6-0 despite, at first, disparaging it. Back in the south he saw the point of going to six axles but, when he turned out such an engine, it was not a new Cardean. The Caledonian locomotive was a conventional 4-4-0 stretched to 4-6-0 with two inside cylinders. Drummond went straight to four cylinders, the cylinder and valve layout operated by Stephenson gear inside but by Walschearts outside (F13 class). These were five very large, 6 foot engines with nearly 2,800 sq. ft total heating surface and 31.5 sq. ft grates. The nominal tractive effort of 25,400 lbs suggests a powerful machine well-advanced on the less than 18,000 lbs of the L12. If only. They were hopeless failures, sluggish on the road, heavy on coal and water and expensive to maintain[37]. A rebuild, the E14, does not appear to have done very much running at all. Just about all the five types of 4-6-0 that Dugald built up to 1912 showed very little improvement. The G14 and P14 classes had outside piston valves and inside slide valves and, although they coped about adequately on the work for which they were designed, they needed skilful handling to stop the fire fragmenting. On the T14 a more or less conventional layout was used, with the outside Walschearts driving the inside cylinders through rocking levers. On these locomotives the smokebox saddle was extended to incorporate the cylinders, giving the front end a massive appearance; with the huge combined splasher boxes, the nickname 'Paddlebox' was more than appropriate. The T14 was the best of Drummond's 4-6-0s, though the word is very much relative. The major drawback to all these locomotives was that they were over-cylindered; their long shallow fireboxes, difficult to keep hot, were poor gas producers that neither superheating nor any other device could do much to improve. That some of the T14s lasted into BR days I find extraordinary.

The use of four cylinders was clearly not necessary. Peter Drummond's Castle class were two-cylinder machines that worked the Scottish gradients perfectly satisfactorily. There was simply no need to complicate the front end, with additional cylinders and sets of valve gear making demands that the boiler could not satisfy. The development of the D15, a much enlarged 4-4-0, was obviously a direct result of the failure of these engines, which, with the other LSWR Drummond four coupleds, outlasted the 4-6-0s by more than a decade. If it had been possible, Dugald would have been better off asking his brother for the loan of a Castle; it would have been far more beneficial than anything of a similar nature that he built himself. After his death, Urie showed comprehensively that a well-designed two cylinder engine, even without large diameter, long travel valves, could operate satisfactorily on LSWR lines.

The facts in the matter of Dugald Drummond's death are well known. In 1912, scalded by boiling water in an accident at Eastleigh, he refused to have the burns properly treated with the result that they went gangrenous, for which the only recourse was amputation. In a last defiant act of arrogance he refused an anaesthetic and died of shock. His brother, it has already been noted, became CME of the Glasgow & South Western in 1912. In his first years at Kilmarnock Peter was not popular; he demanded that his wishes be followed without demur and there were repeated threats of dismissal for those who ignored that instruction.[38] Given that he may not have been like that on the Highland, one can only assume that his arrival at Kilmarnock was not generally welcomed. His uneven career on the HR must have been known to both GSWR officers and running staff; whispers about his adequacy for the appointment may very well have been the underlying cause of this need to impress his will on subordinates. Clearly his brother's 4-6-0s were the major inspiration for a four-cylinder 4-6-0 ascribed to him as being drawn out in 1914.[39] With four 16 inch cylinders and 175 lbs boiler pressure, it appears woefully under-boilered. The GSW can certainly be glad that money was not wasted on it. Peter died in 1918, after 'a short illness'. Thus ended the saga of the Drummond brothers, a tale of adequacy with brief moments of spectacle, sadly.

Chapter 6

Richard Deeley and Cecil Paget

About thirty years ago, a locomotive engineer with whom I was corresponding, referred to a colleague as 'an intellectual but not a very enterprising one'. It is a fact that, against what was quite common in France, where some railway engineers held academic positions, few of Britain's engine designers could be described as intellectuals. Our locomotive engineers, for the most part, learnt on the job from their apprenticeship upwards, about mathematics and science at classes outside their place of work, and what they picked up from rivals or thought they knew anyway. That is not to abuse them, for a profound appreciation of reality, 'street cred' in modern parlance, is essential for the proper advancement of technology. That said, there is also a need to think in terms of the next step but two, and very few of our locomotive designers seem to have been capable of that, albeit sometimes because they were prevented from so doing by factors outside their control.

Cecil Paget is an example of another type of intellectual, one whose thinking was not just advanced on contemporary practice but in some senses disconnected from it. This may have been his downfall. It has long been believed that it was this advanced thinking that led him into dispute with another intellectual, one who, given the opportunity, might have created a rather different Midland Railway to the one that became part of the LMS. This was Richard Deeley, whose proposed four-cylinder compound 4-6-0 remains one of the most interesting locomotives never to have been built. Laid out similarly to the typical French compound – that is, replicating the Crampton influence in French practice – with a possible tractive effort of 25,700 lbs, grate area of 30 sq. ft and an adhesive weight of about 57 tons, it was potentially the equal of Churchward's Star 4-6-0. But it was never built; it is usually claimed that, instead, Derby was engaged in the construction of Paget's sleeve-valved 2-6-2, of which more anon.

Richard Mountford Deeley was born on 24 October 1855. He has been described as being 'possessed of an erudite and very scientific turn of mind' but also as 'a shadowy figure' and to a surprising extent this last comment is true.[1] What we know about his background and family life is almost all based on what he wrote in his majestic work on his family's genealogy.[2] Deeley's father had been involved in the Stourbridge glass trade at the Dial Glassworks until about the time of the Crimean War, when it was forced into closure. He then entered the accounts department of the Midland Railway and later became secretary to the Hydraulic Engineering Co. of Chester. This is where Richard was born, the eldest of three sons and three daughters. At the age of eighteen he became a pupil of the managing director of the Hydraulic Engineering Company and in 1874 was selected to participate in the design of the Brotherhood three-cylinder hydraulic engine. This was a radial engine with the cylinders set at 120°, driving a single crankshaft. It could be powered by air or water power, in which form large numbers were used in marine engineering driving, among other things, capstans. More importantly, a version was developed using steam as its power source. With a radial engine layout the conventional arrangements for the operation of the valves could not be used and the system adopted, in some respects, replicated the uniflow cylinder design. With a reliable high-pressure, steam raising boiler, this had application in the developing technology of road steam vehicles, at that time much advanced on the internal combustion engine.

Deeley was never married and after he left the MR lived alone in a capacious residence in Derby, devoting himself to the study of geology and meteorology.[3] As far as engineering was concerned, he collaborated with Archbutt, the MR chemist, on a 599-page treatise on lubricants and their use, which ran to five editions.[4] Clearly he was no ordinary railway engineer and we may safely assume that Deeley made a useful contribution to the development of the Brotherford engine and that this was important in his selection in 1876 by Johnson as a pupil because he was almost immediately put on to experimental work.

Midland locomotive design has been described by a former Derby apprentice as being

…immersed in the prehistoric past … Every Midland engine was (and is) just about as hot box prone as ingenuity can make it. That was achieved by making the bearings as small as possible, and by fitting a loose brass which added to the knock. .. Midland cylinder and front end design can only be described as appalling, (with the sole exception of the 999 4-4-os which were broken up in a hurry!) Small, short travel piston valves, allied to the most tortuous ports and passages that the foundry could cast, ensured that steam had as difficult a job as human ingenuity could devise to get in and out of the cylinders.[5]

A similar view emanates from no less a person than my father, who wrote,

The locomotive shortage was acute [in 1944] and for working stopping goods trains between Didcot and Reading, or Didcot and Swindon, we were given old Midland Johnson 0-6-0 tender engines. These locomotives were a nightmare to GWR men. No doubt, in their day they had done some good work on the Midland, but to us they were always a source of unreliability and uncertainty.[6]

Johnson is often seen as the origin of these criticisms in that his locomotive policy was very regressive but I do not see that claim as being justified.

Deeley became Chief Clerk of the test department at Derby in March 1890. Three years later, he moved to be Inspector of Boilers, Engines and Machinery, beginning a close association with Johnson. Though he kept in touch with Testing, its chief from 1900 was Henry Fowler. From the beginning of 1902 Deeley was Derby Works Manager and a year later was appointed, additionally, electrical engineer. This appointment is further evidence that Johnson was not living in some kind of technological primordial swamp. The Liverpool–Southport–Crossens–Ormskirk 630V dc electrification programme was planned during his last years in office even if it was not completed until 1913.[7] July 1902 saw Deeley given a further job, as Assistant Locomotive Superintendent; there must have been some awareness of the increasing load being placed on his shoulders for Cecil Paget, Assistant Works Manager at Derby from the beginning of 1902, became Acting Works Manager at Deeley's promotion.[8]

Paget was much younger than Deeley, having been born in October 1874. Deeley had been forty-seven on taking over the management of Derby Works; Paget was only twenty-eight. Yet, in reality, senior railway workshop management, certainly in those years, was a relatively young man's position; to mention only a few, Dugald Drummond was twenty-seven, Webb twenty-five and Churchward thirty-seven when they reached this level. Deeley's 'wait' for works manager may very well have been for nothing other than that Johnson, in office for thirty years, was a logjam to his juniors' progression. For all that, it may have rankled. Paget was educated at Harrow and Pembroke College, Cambridge. Kenneth H. Leech, who numbered him among his close friends, wrote,

> A man of such organizing ability, almost to the amount of genius, full of energy and fun, hidden behind a 'poker face', it is not surprising that tales of his exploits, and incidents in which he was involved are numerous. He was popularly supposed to have suffered more 'swishings' for pranks while at Harrow than any before or since.[9]

As an undergraduate he once met his old headteacher, Dr Welldon; Leech recounts the following possibly apocryphal exchange:

> 'I'm Paget, sir, perhaps you don't remember me?'
>   'Oh yes I do, Paget, but your face is perhaps not the feature I should recognise best.'

He was apprenticed to Johnson at Derby, where, to quote Leech again, '... by influence and ability [he was] soon well on the way to high official position, his youthful exuberance having been – partly at all events – sublimated to the hard work and driving force so characteristic of him'.[10] Note that reference to influence, it is important.

When Deeley took over as Locomotive Superintendent at the beginning of 1904, Paget was confirmed as Works Manager and Assistant Locomotive Superintendent. What actually happened during the next five or so years has been the subject of a great deal of authorship, not a lot of it very definitive. A factor that has always seemed to me to be relevant is that, among most sections of the workforce at Derby, Paget was an outsider. In 1906 he married Lady Alexandra Osborne, fourth daughter of the 9th Duke of Leeds, and they lived in a palatial residence far removed from the kind of official dwelling occupied by similar middle-ranking MR officers. On the other hand, evidence suggests that Paget was far from being an uncaring aristocrat.

As far as relations in the locomotive superintendent's department go, we have very little information about the day-to-day conduct of affairs between Deeley and Paget. The evidence actually suggests that they had originally worked together amicably for, among other things, they went to the USA together to study American workshop practice.[11] Going forward to much later, from 1915 Paget was the lieutenant-colonel commanding a transport company operating around Boulogne; by 1918 there were 25,000 men under his command, but he refused promotion to the rank of brigadier or general because it would have meant moving in with General Staff. He preferred to live with his men, in his own sixteen-coach train, which was moved around behind the front line as circumstances demanded.[12] He took only four hours' sleep, from 02.00 to 06.00, and immediately on rising ran double the length of his train in his pyjamas. Leech said that he '...expected his officers to be able to cook which he could himself', being 'an "epicure of epicures" and "cordon bleu"'.[13] That does not read like a man likely to cause, even unintentionally, conflict with others.

In his book on the Midland Railway,[14] Hamilton Ellis states that 'he had a special hankering for the loco superintendent's job'. Whether that was anything more than a normal ambition to try out his own ideas we do not know, but the *Locomotive Magazine*[15] announced that Paget had indeed been appointed. The source of its announcement is not known but there is a story that has gone the rounds for many years that Johnson let slip that his successor was to be Paget and the fact that Deeley was appointed meant that there was little cordiality or good fellowship between them. Can we hazard the guess that, indeed, Johnson had got it right, that Paget was to be the appointed man? The point here is that he was the son of the Midland's Chairman, Sir George Paget; that worthy might very well have informed Johnson that this was the appointment that he intended to make. Again, it is only a guess but not outside the realms of possibility that other directors brought pressure to bear, privately, on the basis of nepotism. Deeley had, by assiduous attention to his duties, worked his way into the top man's job; he would have been entitled to object to the appointment over his head of an assistant who was in every way less experienced. Nepotism, as opposed to the fairly well known phenomenon of patriarchs and siblings following each other through an organisation, is fundamentally unjust, and Paget senior could not have avoided that being pointed out. That Paget was later promoted to a position above Deeley is not relevant at this stage.

Thus, from this point on, unable to advance his own ideas from within the Midland's locomotive department, he did so privately, as only a rich man could.

Johnson's thirty years as Locomotive Superintendent had produced many noteworthy designs for the MR. His 4-2-2 express locomotives, ninety-five of which were built between 1887 and 1900, were magnificent machines, capable of hauling 250 tons on the mainline between St Pancras and Leicester without difficulty.[16] Of all the late-built single wheelers, these could be said to have been the one type allowed to achieve a normal service life. They were never altered in any way, either by Deeley or Fowler, although there was a proposal to rebuild them as Belpaire 4-4-0s with 7 foot and 6 foot 6 inch driving wheels, first put up in 1906 but cancelled in 1911. The last remained in service until 1928, very nearly the last single to work in Britain.

A rather different type of locomotive was added to stock as a result of a severe shortage of manufacturing capacity at Derby and among manufacturers. To fill the gap, the Midland, Great Northern and Great Central had recourse to order locomotives from American builders. Ten came from that company and a further thirty from Baldwin. Both were typical American 2-6-0s with outside cylinders in which half the smokebox saddle was cast integral with one cylinder block, the exact arrangement adopted by Churchward. With 5 foot driving wheels and a nominal tractive effort of about 19,000 lbs, they were generally comparable to the Midland's own 0-6-0s. Inevitably, the question arises as to whether Derby learnt anything from the American 2-6-0s and the answer, sadly, is not a lot. The access to moving parts was far better than on most contemporary British locomotives, and the cylindrical smoke box was vastly superior to the wrapper type in which the tube plate and front smokebox wall were extended to form its own saddle. In fact, there seems to have been a general prejudice against them right from the start.

Johnson of course is always associated with the Midland's compound 4-4-0s, given the home experience with compounds, easily the most successful built in Britain. Coming as they did right at the time when their near neighbour and rival the LNWR was frustrated beyond endurance with compounds, their take up at Derby is remarkable. The impetus seems to have come from the friendship between Johnson and William M. Smith, who had first worked with him on the Edinburgh & Glasgow Railway and

Daniel Gooch.

Centaur was one of the last batch of Fire Fly 2-2-2s delivered from Nasmyth, Gaskell & Co. in December 1841. Seen here with the original four-wheel tender and guard's 'coffin' seat. These locomotives handled all the best trains on the broad gauge until the building of the Iron Duke class. *Centaur* ran until 1867 but was not actually taken out of service until 1870. (Great Western Trust)

The first of Gooch's 'colossal' locomotives was the 8 foot 2-2-2 *Great Western*, completed in April 1846. There was too much weight on the leading axle, which broke while it was hauling a Down train near Shrivenham. This incident is often quoted but it evokes a good deal of interest beyond that bald fact. For example, it would be interesting to know how, in the years before the electric telegraph, the news was transmitted to Swindon (the nearest available locomotive department) and a rescue engine provided. *Great Western* was rebuilt as a 2-2-2-2 and continued to work until 1870. It retained the Haycock firebox until withdrawn. (Great Western Trust)

The most famous of all broad gauge locomotives was the *Lord of the Isles*, a later Iron Duke locomotive delivered from Swindon Works in March 1851 and seen here in all its glory. That fame obviously has nothing to do with the fact that, in October 1852, when hauling the first train on the Birmingham line, it ran into the back of a preceding train at Aynho! Withdrawn in 1884, it was sent to exhibitions in Edinburgh in 1890, Chicago in 1893 and Earls Court in 1897, between times being kept with *North Star* at Swindon, until the vandals came for it in 1906. (Great Western Trust)

The ten Waverley class locomotives were delivered in 1855. This is *Rob Roy*, with guard's coffin seat, which ran until 1872. The sandwich frames are behind the driving wheels, a format introduced with the 1846 Prince class. It is often claimed that Churchward's 4-6-0s overturned a long GWR tradition of covering that engines' driving wheels in the manner of a Victorian lady covering her legs. If that is so, then this is nudity defined! Despite being described as such, they were not 4-4-0s because the leading wheels were rigid within the frame and not a bogie. The 18 foot wheelbase was only 2 feet shorter than the driving wheelbase of the 47xx 2-8-0s. (Great Western Trust)

This extraordinary photograph was recently discovered by David Castle. It shows *Lord of the Isles* and *North Star* in the spring shop at Swindon. No date is available as to when it was taken but the garb of the man at right suggests the 1890s. There is a cover over *North Star*, presumably to protect it from whatever work is being done on the scaffolding clearly visible above. (Courtesy David Castle)

In 1985 a part-replica of the *Iron Duke* was built under the auspices of the National Rail Museum to mark the 150th anniversary of the GWR. It is not strictly speaking a replica because the boiler came from an Austerity 0-6-0 and the outside axle boxes are dummies. In 2005 the Great Western Society completed a very long term project to build a replica of *Fire Fly*. In 2013 the two engines came together at Didcot, where *Iron Duke* is to remain for the foreseeable future; this is the first time that two broad gauge locomotives have been seen together since 1906. (L. A. Summers)

Thomas Russell Crampton.

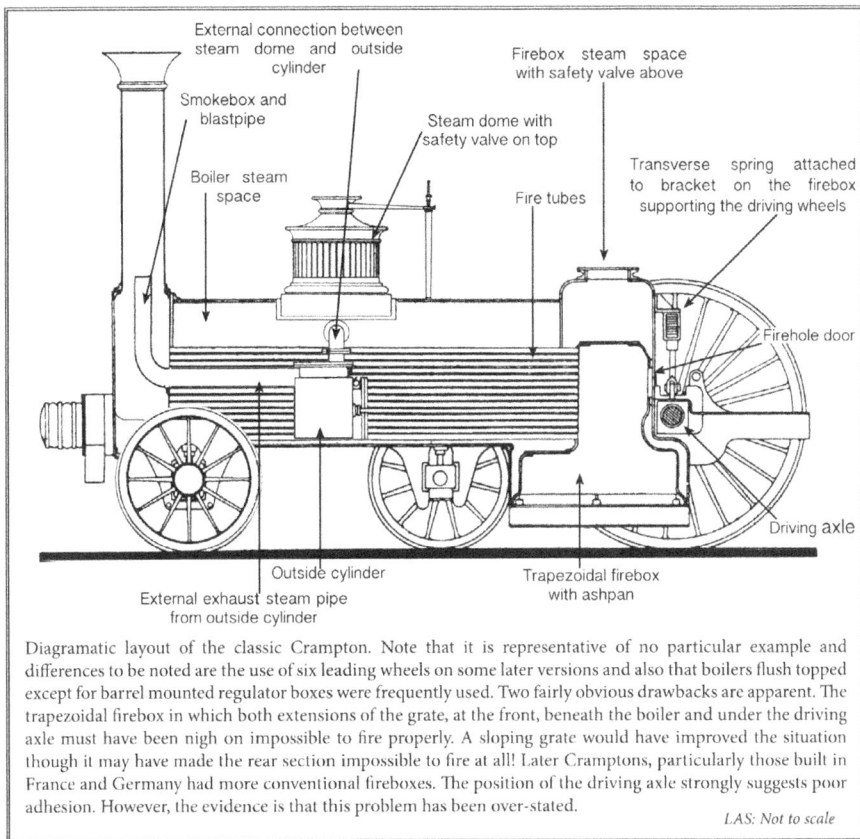

Diagramatic layout of the classic Crampton. Note that it is representative of no particular example and differences to be noted are the use of six leading wheels on some later versions and also that boilers flush topped except for barrel mounted regulator boxes were frequently used. Two fairly obvious drawbacks are apparent. The trapezoidal firebox in which both extensions of the grate, at the front, beneath the boiler and under the driving axle must have been nigh on impossible to fire properly. A sloping grate would have improved the situation though it may have made the rear section impossible to fire at all! Later Cramptons, particularly those built in France and Germany had more conventional fireboxes. The position of the driving axle strongly suggests poor adhesion. However, the evidence is that this problem has been over-stated.

LAS: Not to scale

Kinnaird, No. 14 of the Dundee, Perth & Aberdeen Joint Railway, was probably identical to *Namur* and *Liége* constructed by Tulk & Ley, with three other locomotives, the first Cramptons to be built. They were 4-2-0 (or 2-2-2-0) inside framed types with 7 foot driving wheels. (The late Peter Treloar's Collection/GWT)

Constructed by Bury, Curtis & Kennedy in 1848, 4-2-2-0 *Liverpool* was a much bigger engine than all those that had gone before. It represented Crampton's belief that the power of the larger broad gauge locomotives could be matched on a standard gauge chassis. Despite its reputation, the author believes that on lighter trains *Liverpool* performed perfectly adequately. (L. A. Summers Collection)

One of the celebrated 2-2-2-0 Cramptons built by Derosne & Cail for the Nord Railway in 1849. The significance of the design was the large diameter steam pipes in which the ratio to the piston area was 1:8.4, greater than any locomotive until the arrival of the Nord compound 4-4-0s in 1892. (L. A. Summers Collection)

The sole surviving original German Crampton locomotive is *Phoenix*, built by Hauptwerkstatte-Karlsruhe in 1863 for the Baden Railway. It ran until 1903. (L. A. Summers)

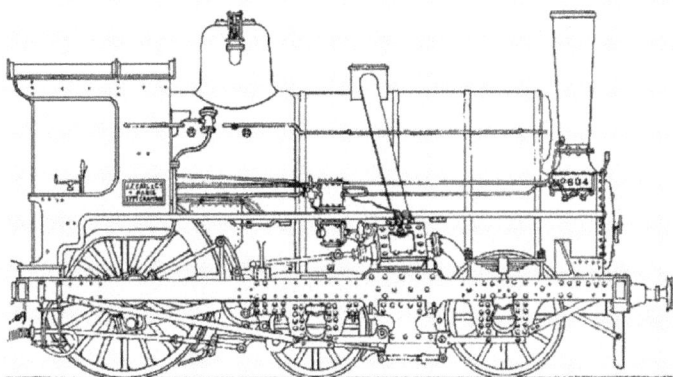

Left: Est Crampton No 604 rebuilt with Flaman double barrel boiler, 1889. Below: An old photograph of a Salomon Est 4-4-0 with Flaman double barrel boiler. The locomotives looks very unweildy but they ran successfully for many years.
Both: L A Summers collection

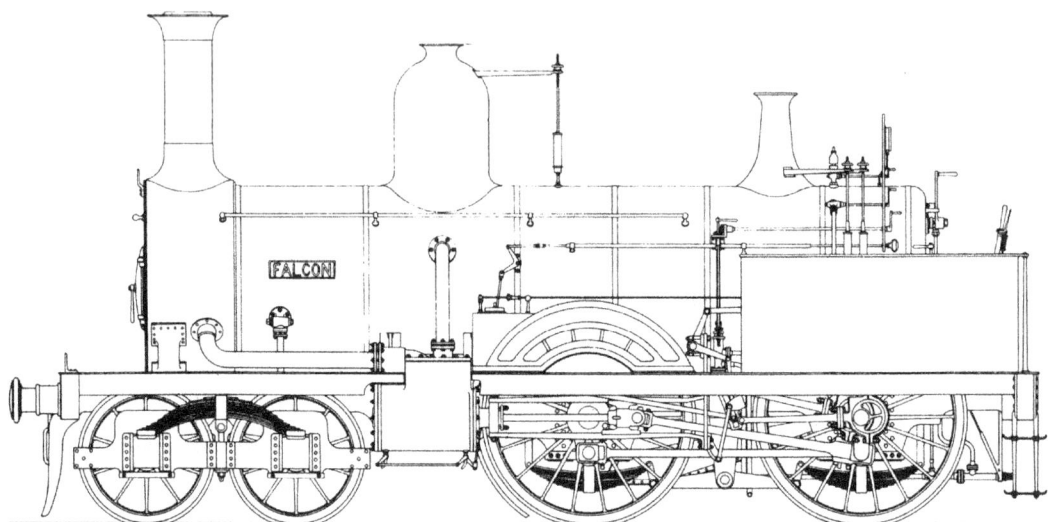

London, Chatham & Dover Railway Tiger class 4-4-0 *Falcon*, intended for general passenger work and delivered from Hawthorn & Co. in 1861. The Locomotive Superintendent of the LC&DR, William Martley was an ex-GWR divisional manager and this may have prejudiced him against Crampton. He was bitterly opposed to these locomotives being ordered and, after several incidents while running, they were rebuilt as 2-4-0s. Whether all the incidents were due to the locomotives rather than the poor quality of the track is an open question. (Drawn by Len Ward for the RCTS and published here with kind permission)

A very old postcard picture of LCDR Echo class 4-4-0 No. 29. Originally delivered from Robert Stephenson & Co. in 1862 as an intermediate drive locomotive with a boiler similar to the Tiger class, reconstructing it as a 4-4-0 involved little more than substituting a driving axle for the intermediate shaft and fitting a connecting rod. Note that the bogie is similar to that seen on *Falcon*. (The late Peter Treloar's Collection/GWT)

Charles R. Sacré.

The early form of
the Sacré 2-4-0, with
6 foot driving wheels.
These were the express
passenger engines on the
line until the larger 2-4-0s
came out in 1873. (Late
Peter Treloar's Collection/
GWT)

The later version of the
Sacré 2-4-0, as running
in Great Central days,
with a Robinson chimney.
Note the 'port hole' cab
side window. (Late Peter
Treloar's Collection/
GWT)

Sacre's 6B 4-4-0 No. 423 in original condition apart from the substitution of the original chimney with Pasher's ugly stove pipe. The characteristic cab with a small oval 'port hole' window between the side sheet cut-out and the front of the cab first appeared on these locomotives. (R. M. Casserley Collection)

A 6B 4-4-0 in Great Central days, now numbered 438b and seen at Trafford Park (Manchester) shed. It has acquired an extended smokebox and Robinson chimney but is otherwise unaltered. (R. M. Casserley Collection)

Class 14 2-2-2 No. 108, built for the MS&L-operated Cheshire Lines Committee route from Manchester to Liverpool and shown as running in Great Central days. Ahrons is very complimentary to the class, describing them as remarkably powerful and able to start heavy trains well. The location is Trafford Park shed, Manchester. (R. M. Casserley Collection)

Patrick Stirling.

An impression of Patrick Stirling's Class 40 2-2-2s for the Glasgow & South Western Railway, built 1860. The cab is probably derived from Jane Stirling's cardboard model, while the overall appearance shows the early style of the characteristic Stirling locomotive appearance. (L. A. Summers)

A later version of the GNR Stirling 2-2-2, No. 874, was built in 1892. The fan-shaped splasher holes have been abandoned but the distinctive Stirling appearance is otherwise unchanged. These engines had 7 foot, 7½ inch driving wheels and worked in the same rosters as the 4-2-2s. (R. M. Casserley Collection)

GNR No. 76 is representative of more than 150 0-4-2 tender engines built for freight work by Patrick Stirling between 1868 and 1895 with little variation in dimensions. Sometimes used on passenger trains, their low-power boilers did permit heavy, fast running. (The Late Peter Treloar's Collection/GWT)

One of the 1894 series of Great Northern Stirling 'eight footers', No. 1003 was photographed in July 1909. These were the most powerful and heaviest of the type but for some reason were not used in the 1895 'Race to the North'. They spent their last years on the level lines in Lincolnshire. (The Late C. Laundy/ GWT)

LAS after JNM

It is not often remembered that Stirling '8 footer' No. 1 was not, at first, as successful as suggested by the reputation that the class later gained. While its shortcomings were being examined, the chief draughtsman sketched out a 4-4-0 proposal that, inevitably, Stirling refused to approve. The drawing was, not surprisingly, lost to sight until the 1950s. It clearly demonstrates what a P. Stirling 4-4-0 would have looked like, should he have ever been pushed into designing one. (L. A. Summers after the Late J. N. Maskelyne)

Looking ex-works, James Stirling's F Class 4-4-0 No. A210 is seen at Ramsgate in 1928. Built in 1886, No. 210 was one of the few of this class not rebuilt as an F1 and was scrapped in 1930. The generally pleasing appearance of the engine is ruined by the positioning of the uncovered Ramsbottom safety valves. (H. C. Casserley)

At Ashford in August 1925, James Stirling's B Class 4-4-0 No. A458 looks as though a good clean would be in order. Despite the impression created by the substitution of the Stirling cab by something more commodious, the general appearance of the engine is still spoilt by the position of the safety valves. One of only two B class locomotives not rebuilt to B1, most of which lasted into BR days, No. 458 was scrapped in 1931. (H. C. Casserley)

Mathew Stirling's J class express passenger 4-4-0s were built for the Hull & Barnsley Railway from 1910. LNER No. 2428 is seen at Botanic Garden (Hull) shed in June 1931 after having been rebuilt with a NER domed boiler. They were probably surplus to LNER needs; kept in store for several years, the last was scrapped in 1934. (H. C. Casserley)

Dugald (top) and Peter Drummond.

Caledonian 4-2-2 No. 123 as LMS 14010 and running with its third boiler. It is likely that this engine was 'Drummond designed' only in that his chief draughtsman, collaborating with his opposite number at Neilson & Co., encouraged the adoption of as many of his master's ideas as possible. Restored to the condition in which it ran in 1958, No. 123 is now preserved in the Glasgow Riverside Museum. (The Late Peter Treloar's Collection/GWT)

Eglinton was the 4-4-0 built by Dubs & Co. to stand alongside 4-2-2 No. 123 at the Edinburgh Exhibition of 1886, at which it was awarded a gold medal. It was essentially a Drummond Class 66 locomotive but with larger cylinders and other refinements. Becoming Caledonian No. 124, it was rebuilt in 1887 and named in 1890. *Eglinton* continued to work until 1925. (The Late Peter Treloar's Collection/GWT)

Peter Drummond's Small Ben class for the Highland Railway. No. 10 *Ben Slioch* was built in 1899 and was photographed in what was probably the usual running conditions of all engines in the early years of the twentieth century. The Small Bens spent most of their lives working the northern lines between Inverness and Wick and on the through trains to Aberdeen. (The Late Peter Treloar's Collection/GWT)

Highland Railway 4-6-0 No. 143 *Gordon Castle*, built 1900. Although constructed during the tenancy of Peter Drummond at Lochgorm, the Castles were clearly not due to his detailed design work and were derived from the express passenger 4-6-0 left on the drawing board when David Jones was forced to retire in 1896. They were highly successful and remained at work until 1947. (R. M. Casserley Collection)

Dugald and Peter Drummond: 4-4-0 dimensions

Year	Railway	Class	Cyldrs	Boiler heatg sf	Boiler length	Boiler diamtr	pressure	grate	Driving wheel	Bogie wheel	Engine weight	Tractive effort	Designer
1876	NBR	476	18x26	1099.3		4'5⅛"	140	21	6'6"		46/2	12852	DDrummond
1884	Cal	66	18x26	1208.6	10'7"		150	19	6'6"	3'6"		14720	DD
1886	Cal	Eglinton	18x26*	1208.6			150	19	6'6"	3'6"		14720	DD
1888	Cal	Gourock Bogies	18x26	963.5			150		5'9"	3'6"		15567	DD
1898	LSWR	C8	18½x26	1191.6	10'6"	4'5"	175	20.36	6'7"	3'7"		16756	DD
1898	Highl'd	Small Ben	18¼x26	1178	10'6"	4'6¼	175	20¼	6'0"	3'6"	46/17	17890	PDrummond
1899	LSWR	T9	18½x26	1499.7§	10'6"	4'5"	175	24	6'7"	3'7"	48/2	17670	DD
1901	LSWR	K10	18½x26	1291.0	10'6"	4'5"	175	20.36	5'7"	3'7"	46/14	19756	DD
1903	LSWR	S11	19x26	1550.0	10'6"	5'0"	175	24	6'1"	3'7"	52	19400	DD
1904	LSWR	L11	18½x26	1500.0	10'6"	4'5"	175	24	5'7"	3'7"	51	17756	DD
1904	LSWR	L12	19x26	1550.0	10'6"	5'0"	175	24	6'7"	3'7"	53/19	17673	DD
1908	Highl'd	Large Ben	18¼x26	1648.2	10'6"	5'3"	180	20¼	6'0"	3'6"	53/30	18401	PD
1912	LSWR	D15	19½x26	1724.0	12.00	5'0"	200	27	6'7"	3'7"	59/15	22333	DD
1913	GSWR	131	19½x26				180		6'0"	3'6"		21009	PD
1915	GSWR	137	19½x26			5'3"	180		6'0"	3'6"	52	21009	PD

Dugald Drummond 4-2-2-0 Double Singles

Year	Railway	Class	Cyldrs	heatg sf	length	diamtr	pressure	grate	Driving wheel	Bogie wheel	weight
1897	LSWR	T7	(4)15x26	1664.0	12'00"	4'5"	175	27.4	6'7"	3'7"	54/11
	New boiler put on 1904			1760.0	12'00	5'0"	175	27.4			60/1
1901	LSWR	E10	(4)14x26	1690.0	12'00"	4'5"	175	27.4	6'7"	3'7"	57/15

* Originally 19" with Joy valve gear

§ The T9 and all succeeding LSWR 4-4-0s, class E10 and the new boiler put on the T7 had water tubes in the firebox. The figures quoted here *include* between 100 and 170 square feet of additional heating surface thus provided. Peter Drummond used water tubes in the fireboxes of certain of his 0-6-0s but not on 4-4-0s despite their being included in the abortive 1901 proposal.

Dimensions expressed: Cylinders in inches, boiler heating surface and grate area in square feet; boiler length and diameter in feet and inches; pressure in lbs/square inch; wheels in feet and inches; weight in long tons and cwts; tractive effort in lbs.

Where a box in the diagram above is blank, the author has been unable to reliably establish the correct dimensional figure.

Peter Drummond's 'Austrian Goods' 2-6-0s were built for the Glasgow & South Western in 1915. Claimed to be very economical runners, they were used on heavy goods trains between Glasgow and Carlisle. The unofficial class name was a result of their being built from material purchased by North British for an Austrian order received just before the outbreak of the First World War. (The Late Peter Treloar's Collection/GWT)

Dugald Drummond's second mixed traffic 4-4-0 series for the LSWR, the K10 class first appeared in 1901. Lively, versatile machines, they were known as 'Grasshoppers'. No. 152 was built in 1902 and is seen here in Southern Railway days, after removal of the firebox water tubes, sometime in the 1930s. The last K10 worked until 1951. (The Late Peter Treloar's Collection/GWT)

Possibly conceived as a non-compound version of Webb's double singles, Drummond's 4-2-2-0 locomotives of both T7 and E10 classes were no more successful, the uncoupled driving wheels being a serious drawback. All were withdrawn from service early in the Southern era. (The Late Peter Treloar's Collection/GWT)

Dugald Drummond's 4-6-0s for the LSWR must be among the most unsatisfactory series of locomotives ever built in Britain. The T14 class, known as 'Paddleboxes' because of the large splasher boxes, were probably the best of a bad bunch, employed on the Waterloo, Southampton and Bournemouth trains. (The Late Peter Treloar's Collection/GWT)

Urie later rebuilt the T14 class 4-6-0s with superheaters, extended smokeboxes and new fireboxes without the water tubes so beloved by Drummond. The Southern later rebuilt them again, most noticeably by raising the level of the footplate, abolishing the paddleboxes and thus improving access. In this photograph of No. 445 some wag has chalked the name 'Flying Fox' on the centre driving wheel splasher. (The Late Peter Treloar's Collection/GWT)

R. M. Deeley (upper) and C. W. Paget.

The famous Johnson 'Spinner' 4-2-2, probably the most famous of all Midland Railway locomotive classes. No. 665 was built in 1896 and is seen here in May 1924, displaying the early LMS livery, at Kentish Town shed. By this time they were used mainly on local stopping trains and as station pilots. (H. C. Casserley)

Johnson compound No. 2635 in original condition. This engine differed slightly from the first two, most noticeably in that the footplating ran straight over the cylinder without being raised. Later renumbered 1004, it was rebuilt as a Deeley compound and superheated in 1904. (R. M. Casserley Collection)

The LMS 1924 Compounds differed from the Deeley design in little more than the reduction of the driving wheels from 7 feet to 6 feet, 9 inches in diameter. An unidentified member of this group makes a fine sight with an express from St Pancras to Manchester. (The late Peter Treloar's Collection/GWT)

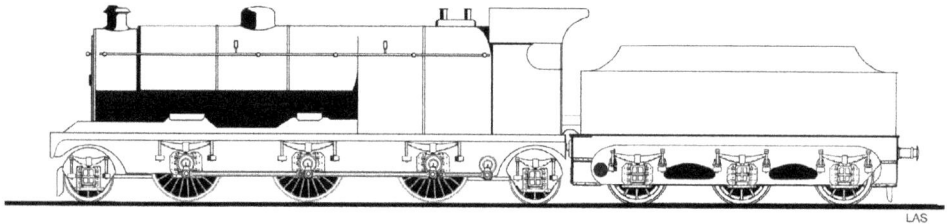

This new drawing of the Paget 2-6-2 locomotive brings out the large sized boiler and the commodious cab. Note the short throw cranks on the connecting rod and the unusual position of the springs. Normal practice was to lengthen the hangers so that the springs were positioned above the level of the footplate. (Drawing by L. A. Summers)

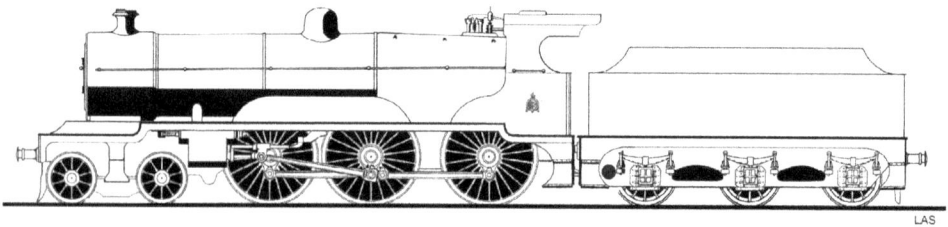

Deeley's four-cylinder compound 4-6-0 proposal, an outline based on the original Sandham Symes drawing, itself the only extant evidence for the design. In many respects it is a pity that the work was not progressed; with its weaknesses developed out it might have been a very successful locomotive, giving a new life to the British compound. (Drawing by L. A. Summers)

Deeley 999 Class 4-4-0 No. 808 (originally 998) at Derby in June 1926. Rather than prejudice, it is more likely that their relatively early scrapping was due to the non-standard Stevart valve gear, which was difficult to set up. (H. C. Casserley)

Richard Maunsell.

Borsig-built Class L 4-4-0 No. 31773 is seen at Tonbridge shed after Nationalisation. The ten members of this class were delivered only a few weeks before the outbreak of the First World War but on its conclusion the payment for their construction was scrupulously made to their German manufacturer. (Frank Hornby)

The three-cylinder version of the River class 2-6-4T was No. A890 *River Frome*, completed in December 1925. Note the link running from the motion across the face of the cylinder to the conjugate gear ahead of the cylinders. Although this was superior to the Gresley layout, it imposed a quite different restraint on servicing and maintenance. It ran in this condition only until the Sevenoaks disaster, when it was taken out of service and later rebuilt as tender engine. (Great Western Trust)

This is a modern photograph of preserved locomotives but it provides a useful comparison between the standard GWR Mogul (No. 5322) and the Maunsell type derived from it. BR 31806 was built originally as a River class 2-6-4T in October 1926, No. A806 *River Torridge*. It was rebuilt as a U class 2-6-0 tender engine in 1928. In 1957 it was further rebuilt with BR Type 4 cylinders, chimney and blastpipe. (L. A. Summers)

Maunsell's version of the LSWR N15 4-6-0 express locomotive, thirty locomotives originally numbered 763 to 792, built by North British and delivered during 1925. Although retaining the essential Urie appearance, they were much improved with new front end arrangements and a better firebox layout. The SR Board decided to name them after knights associated with the legend of the Round Table, a decision of which Maunsell did not entirely approve; No. 769 was *Sir Balan*. (The late Peter Treloar's Collection/GWT)

The prototype of the Lord Nelson class in almost 'as built' condition. Problems with smoke obscuring the driver's view became a problem with the bigger locomotives built for some railways. This was dealt with by providing a flat shield along the smokebox, creating an airflow that lifted the smoke above the boiler. The downside to this provision was that the impressive appearance of many locomotives was consequently ruined, that certainly being the case with all Maunsell's locomotives. (The late Peter Treloar's Collection/GWT)

Lord Nelson as rebuilt by Bulleid with Lemaitre multiple jet blast pipe and large diameter chimney; this process transformed the performance of the Nelsons, although opinions differ as to the effect it had on their appearance. Bulleid further blotted his copybook by adopting an 'unlovely' livery called malachite green. (L. A. Summers)

The Schools class 4-4-0 has been described as a 'two thirds' Nelson but it does not take much effort to see that there are fundamental differences in the design, particularly the adoption of a round-topped firebox. This was at the insistence of Eastleigh Chief Draughtsman Finlayson, who claimed that the Belpaire type would obscure the driver's vision, a point strongly contested by Holcroft. The Schools were outstandingly successful locomotives. No. 925 was one of the 1934 series and carried the name *Cheltenham*. (Barbara Summers)

Sir Nigel Gresley.

The K3 2-6-0 was the first GNR locomotive to be designed with the standard form of the Gresley gear, the prototype completed in 1920. Intended for fast goods work and often operated at speed on passenger trains, nearly 200 were eventually constructed. (The Late Peter Treloar's Collection/GWT)

Original A1 Pacific No. 4479 *Robert the Devil* makes an impressive sight leaving King's Cross. This was one of the 1923 batch of A1s, actually the tenth to be completed. It was later rebuilt as an A3 and was still working East Coast expresses in the late 1950s. (The Late Peter Treloar's Collection/GWT)

As first restored for preservation in its original 1943 A3 condition, No. 4472 *Flying Scotsman* storms past the photographer on a special steam-hauled train. The third A1 to be built, No. 4472 achieved its reputed 100 mph record run before rebuilding as an A3. (Rebecca J. Shields)

Only two P1 class 2-8-2 freight locomotives were built because, although they could handle 1,600-ton trains, they needed special signal arrangements to do so and they were too powerful for the generality of freight operations. The P1s were originally fitted with A1 boilers and boosters, later removed. The A1 boilers were replaced by the A3 type a few years before they were withdrawn in 1945. (The Late Peter Treloar's Collection/GWT)

The J39 was the 5 foot, 2 inch version of the Gresley 0-6-0, introduced in 1926, together with the 4 foot, 8 inch J39 totaling 325 examples. No. 65929 is seen at Dunfermline in 1966. (L. A. Summers)

Apart from the Schools and the G&SW *Lord Glenarthur*, very few 4-4-0s built in the UK had more than two cylinders and it can be asked what the point was of the D49 class being built in this form. The first thirty-six engines were named after counties (shires) through which the LNER ran, the remainder after fox hunting groups. No. 62712, now preserved, is *Morayshire*. (L. A. Summers)

Gresley's experimental compound water tube boiler 4-6-4 No. 10000, known unofficially as the 'Hush Hush' because of the secrecy that surrounded its construction. Water tube boilers were frequently used in marine boiler design, but do not seem to have been successful on locomotives, possibly because of loading gauge constraints. Although No. 10000 put up some good work and was actually worked in a normal operational link, eventually maintenance and servicing difficulties outweighed any advantage gained. (The Late Peter Treloar's Collection/GWT)

The P2 class Mikados will always be controversial on account of the assertion by Thompson that their performance on the Edinburgh–Aberdeen line was unsatisfactory, and the obvious unwillingness to relocate them to King's Cross for East Coast express work. A more appropriate criticism is that, as a class of only six locomotives, they were hardly standard designs. No. 2002 *Earl Marischal* is seen in an 'inbetween' condition, fitted with disfiguring smoke deflectors. They were all later streamlined after the A4 shape. Note the awful black smoke blotting out the sky. (The Late Peter Treloar's Collection/GWT)

Gresley A4 Pacific *Bittern* in post-war LNER garter blue livery, numbered 19 and making the classic impression. Originally these locomotives had a deep valance over the wheels to counter the turbulence caused by the operation of the valve gear. It was, however, a hindrance to maintenance and removed. Perversely this had the effect of improving their appearance! (L. A. Summers)

Gresley's V2 2-6-2 locomotive, introduced in 1936, was a most significant and successful design. Essentially built for fast mixed traffic they did, over the years, take a full share of express passenger work, as demonstrated by No. 60835 in this photograph taken at Aberdeen in 1964. (L. A. Summers)

went with him to the Great Eastern in 1866. In 1874 Smith went to Japan for nine years as Locomotive Superintendent of the Imperial Government Railways. Smith was only one of well over 100 British professionals who worked in Japan at this time.[17] The foreigners were not always popular and Smith returned to Britain in 1883 to become Chief Draughtsman at Darlington. It was here that the 'Smith compound' was born. The Quaker Wilson Worsdell was actually Locomotive Superintendent but his Chief Draughtsman was much more than just manager of the drawing office. Two-cylinder compounds derived from the von Borries type had been favoured by Wilson's brother, Thomas, but now they were to be reconstructed as simples. When No. 1619, a much celebrated locomotive, was due for conversion, it was, instead, turned out as a three-cylinder compound on the system that has become linked with Smith's name. In contrast to the Webb three-cylinder compound layout, the new No. 1619 had one high-pressure cylinder inside and two low-pressure cylinders outside. Though successful and followed some years later by two 4-4-2 Smith compounds, the NER did not change its overall preference for simple locos.

Johnson and Smith were obviously in contact, and the Midland locomotive engineer was sufficiently interested to try this compound system for himself. He was aided in doing so by another NER man, confusingly also named Smith, J. W., Chief Locomotive Draughtsman at Derby from 1901 to 1906. J. W. Smith may very well have made the principal contribution to the design of these locomotives.[18] The first two compounds started work in January 1902 but both were actually completed before the end of 1901. 4-4-0s with a single high-pressure cylinder 19 inches × 26 inches inside and two low-pressure cylinders 21 inches × 26 inches outside. The exhaust steam from the high-pressure cylinder passed directly via a common steam chest to the low-pressure cylinders. Drive was on the leading axle and three sets of Stephenson gear with six eccentrics were fitted between the frames. The driving wheels were 7 feet in diameter and the adhesive weight 38.9 tons. The total heating surface was 1,719 sq. ft with a 26 foot grate. The driving arrangements were complicated and necessitated the locomotives to be allocated their own enginemen. Without going into details, the complications arose from the operation of valves, which permitted No. 2631 to be worked as a simple, semi-compound or full compound engine, as circumstances required. Usually, working simple was for starting; with a heavy train on a significant gradient, semi-compound mode could be deployed, by which high-pressure steam could be added to the low-pressure steam entering the outside cylinders. British railways never trained their steam enginemen to be technocrats in the way that was the norm in France, where the then-contemporary de Glehn compounds had equally complicated driving arrangements. The remaining three came out in July, September and November 1903. Nos 2632 and 2635 had Serve (corrugated) boiler tubes but these were later removed. There were also detail differences, mainly in the run of the footplating.

Rous Marten had a very exciting run behind one of these engines; we are not told which, though it was probably No. 2631.[19] A 240-ton train comprised the 11.50 Scottish Express from Carlisle to Leeds, booked 138 minutes overall. A punctual start from Carlisle was almost immediately compromised by a 2.5 minute stand just outside Citadel station. On a rising grade 40 mph was reached within two miles, and 45 and above maintained until passing Appleby, 30.75 miles, covered in 34 minutes, 33 seconds. After Appleby, beyond the viaduct, the lines rises to Aisgill. As far as Crosby Garret speed never fell below 45 and then began to rise, a maximum of 53.6 being recorded before it began to fall back. Kirkby Stephen was passed at 47.4 and the summit reached at 43 mph. Overall the time from Carlisle, traversing 48.5 miles and climbing 1,100 feet, to Aisgill was 57 minutes, 38 seconds. It was after Blaemoor that the recorder's pulse began to quicken. Down the 15 mile descent to Settle, speed rose rapidly to 75 mph, then successively at the quarter mile posts past 90 to a maximum of 91.8 mph. Rous Marten adds, 'It does not need much demonstration that this was a very fine piece of locomotive work… reflect[ing] much credit on [Driver] Killan.'[20]

Clearly the Midland had a good engine on its hands but just as clear was the need to revise the design, if for no other reason than to simplify the driving arrangements. Deeley designed a very simple arrangement by which from starting until the regulator reached about 20° of opening, when the speed was about 10 mph, the engine worked simple; as the regulator was opened further, compound working began. Returning to simple working could not be achieved except by pulling the regulator back to the closed position and then opening it again. The boiler was also modified; the boiler pressure was raised to 220 lbs (later reduced to 200) and a larger firebox, with the grate area increased to 28.4 sq. ft, was fitted. Deeley also modified the extraordinary smokebox design. The Johnson compounds had a complicated form of the standard Midland wrapper type, already described, but with a drumhead front tubeplate within a wrapper type internal and external smokebox.[21] Deeley put the smokebox on a separate saddle. The footplate layout was also altered and, with the rear splasher joining the cab side in an elegant curve, an attractive locomotive was achieved. Thirty of this new type were produced in 1905/6 and a further ten in 1908/9. These later engines had extended smokeboxes and other detail alterations. The Johnson originals were rebuilt to confirm with the later versions in 1914. Superheating introduced with these rebuilds did not become general until after 1919. It needs no recording how, after the Grouping in 1923, the LMS built 195 slightly altered versions of these engines, to the chagrin particularly of former LNWR people. For all that, one cannot escape the conclusion reported by E. S. Cox that tests carried out in 1923/25 'establish[ed] the ascendancy of the Midland compound in efficient operation... As against coal consumption of the order of 5lbs/DBHP hour general with simple expansion types on the then LMS, the compound ranged around 4lbs on comparable duties ...'[22]

By 1905, then, Deeley had developed a highly successful locomotive, equal to the tasks required of it by the MR. Though he continued to build developments of the Johnson 4-4-0 simples and 0-6-0 freight engines, his attention turned to more advanced ideas. An 0-8-0 goods engine with outside 20 inch × 26 inch cylinders and 10.5 inch diameter piston valves was drawn up; also an 0-6-2 shunting tank and a 2-6-4T.[23] One other scheme deserves further attention, for it was a compound tank engine of very novel design. Exactly what initiated the proposal, no one has been able to say definitively. The proposal appears to be dated to 1906 and involved mounting the compound 4-4-0 boiler and an all-over cab and bunker ensemble on a 2-4-4-2 chassis with four outside cylinders, the high-pressure pair placed behind the second set of driving wheels and the low-pressure cylinders in the more usual position, ahead of the first set. Thus the high-pressure cylinders were driving forwards and the low-pressure towards the rear. I know of no other British locomotive either proposed or built in this form but there were a couple constructed much later in the USA – in particular, the Baltimore & Ohio 4-4-4-4, *Geo. Emerson* built in 1935. In this locomotive the rear cylinders were placed next to the firebox and it is claimed that the immediate area, hot and dirty, caused premature cylinder wear. On Deeley's engine, the cylinders, placed right back under the bunker, would not have suffered in this way. However, that may have been the crucial flaw in the design. The steam feed pipes both to the high-pressure cylinders and from there forwards to the low-pressure set would have had to travel further than was normally acceptable and would have taken up undue space in the long side tank. What strikes your author is that, although it could have been easily done, the two 'engines' were not linked with a common coupling rod. This would have been protection against the drag at the drawbar of heavy loads reducing the adhesion of the front engine. It would also have permitted at least one set of wheels to have reduced flanges, thus making some easement of the rigid wheelbase. The proposal was never advanced beyond an initial drawing and instead the 0-6-4Ts for ever known as 'Flatirons' were built. Sadly, they were not wholly successful, even when fitted with superheated Belpaire boilers, probably because the steam passages were too complex.

At some point around this time Deeley was also turning his attention to a four-cylinder compound 4-6-0. However, matters now become complicated and, especially in terms of personalities, very difficult to fathom. The Derby team was Deeley and Paget, with, from 1906, James Edward Anderson as Chief Locomotive Draughtsman and Sandham Symes his assistant. Anderson was involved with the proposal just described, but the outline of the 4-6-0 seems to have been the work of Symes.[24] Into the picture now comes the man who, it can be argued, was the real villain of the piece. Guy Granet, the son of a banker and a graduate of Balliol College, was called to the Bar in 1893. In 1900 he took on the post of secretary to the Railway Companies' Association, which he held for five years. Clearly an ambitious man, he came to the attention of the Midland Board, who appointed him Assistant General Manager in 1905. The assistant general managers of the old railways did not necessarily involve themselves in operational matters; more likely he was employed on Parliamentary and legal work, at the same time informing himself of the GM's traffic responsibilities. John Mathieson was the General Manager and on his retirement in 1906 Granet was promoted to take his place. That appointment was crucial, as we shall see.

Paget, denied what he may have been promised – the position of Locomotive Superintendent, undertook to develop his ideas privately, in his own time. Much, if not all, of what we know about this work is due to the man he took on as his employee, James Clayton. Born in 1872 Clayton won the Queen's Prize at what was then the Manchester Technical School and became a draughtsman with Beyer, Peacock and later the SER. In 1904 he worked briefly as Chief Draughtsman, working on engine and transmission design, and as works manager for the Albion Motor Manufacturing Company of Coventry.[25,26] When the company got into financial difficulties, Clayton was out of work until he was taken on by Paget, clearly interested in the contribution that he could make through his experience with internal combustion engines. It is not clear how long he was actually employed by Paget because, according to the record, he was in charge of the casualty and investigation section of the MR from 1904 to 1905, when he became Assistant Chief Locomotive Draughtsman.[27] Clayton wrote nothing publicly about the Paget locomotive until after Deeley's death, contributing an important and detailed technical account of the project to the *Railway Gazette* in 1945.[28]

The starting point for his interest was a fascination with the Willans high-speed central valve engine, which had been installed to produce electrical power for Derby Works offices, and the railway station and proved cheap and economical to run. The essential ingredients of these engines were single acting cylinders with a central spindle valve, a kind of multi-stage piston valve shared between all the related cylinders. This was clearly the attractive point of the engine, reducing the moving parts and therefore wear and tear. Paget's objective was to replicate the principle of the Willans engine in railway locomotive design and thereby create good balance and riding qualities. The first proposal was for a massive 4-6-0 but this was abandoned due, probably, to excessive weight. A second proposal was a 2-6-2 with outside frames, adopted to obtain as much space as possible for the eight single acting cylinders. They were mounted horizontally on the line of the axles, two sets of four between the leading and centre driving axles and the second set between the centre and rear axles. The drive was via trunk pistons: two driving the leading driving axle and two the rear axle, with the central axle driven from four cylinders, two each of the rear-facing cylinders, and the other two from the forward-facing rear set. Steam distribution was controlled by rotary sleeve valve gear, giving rapid opening and closing but requiring little power to operate. The driving wheels were 5 feet, 4 inches in diameter. The adhesion was 58 tons out of a total engine weight of 74 tons. A secondary feature related to one of the most expensive components in the steam engine, the firebox, with its inner and outer walls held rigid by hundreds of stays vulnerable to the change in temperature between the inner wall, the water in the intervening 'water legs' and the external wall. Paget replaced this with one in which the water legs were discarded in favour of firebrick walls, 6 inches deep at the sides and rear and 9 inches at its front. The heating surface was 1,948 sq. ft for the tubes and 70 sq. ft for the firebox. Two firehole doors were provided. The grate area was 33.75 sq. ft. Below the firebox, the uniquely designed ashpan was designed to be self-cleaning.

By the time that the 2-6-2 was under construction, in 1907/8, Paget became aware that his own resources were not going to cover its cost. Despite the fact that his father was still Chairman, he now encountered ill-will with his request that the company should complete the financing of the project. It is claimed that Deeley viewed the locomotive with displeasure and suspicion, seeing his authority circumvented by the agreement to construct it.[29] Thus, from this contention comes the assumption that when the Midland took on the remaining cost of construction, it insisted on taking control of all tests and limiting the amount of experimental work that might prove necessary. Leech says that, '... right from the start Derby had shown the utmost hostility to the new design ... to hand over the machine to such diehards was to destroy any chance of the locomotive's success, unless it should prove to have no teething troubles whatever...'[30] I am not entirely sure that this is as obvious as commentators have suggested, certainly in relation to Deeley. It is possible to argue that the Deeley 4-6-0 was a riposte to the Paget locomotive but the plain fact is that no drawings other than the initial outline for this proposal have been found or indeed are likely to have existed. Therefore, to contend, as some have, that Deeley fumed at the space taken in the works by the Paget engine, where there should be his 4-6-0, is rather ridiculous. Apart from anything else, there was plenty of space in the erecting shops for both locomotives to be constructed concurrently; furthermore the £1,500 required to complete the Paget 2-6-2, even if it came from his budget, could not possibly have been a large percentage of the department's annual expenditure.

Paget's locomotive was completed in January 1909 and, in accordance with the agreement, Derby undertook to run the engine under test. Leech reported that Paget told him that the boiler steamed well and gave no trouble as regards leakage but that there was some trouble with firebrick walls cracking. It ran smoothly, he said, 'like a Spinner' at 80 mph. The only trouble was leakage of steam past the piston rings, which caused a cloud of steam to surround the engine when running slowly, a problem he did not regard as irresolvable.[31] There is no doubt that it ran fast and smoothly on a number of occasions but there were several serious faults that undermined the design. Tuplin noted that firebricks got white hot on inner surfaces and were not much different on the outside, so that a firebrick wall on a locomotive needed to be much thicker than the loading gauge allowed.[32] In fact it was the valves and cylinders that were the Achilles' heel of the design; the difference in expansion of the sleeve valves and liners, manufactured from different metals, caused leakage to an unacceptable degree.[33] The incident in which No. 2299 failed doing 70 through Syston, when a whole sleeve assembly seized up and wrecked itself, causing complete failure with a resulting eight-hour blockage of the line, appears to be a myth. The incident happened off the main line and did not affect the normal traffic. The engine was taken back to Derby by a shunting engine and that is how the trouble occurred. The cylinders, running unlubricated and without steam, got very hot and cracking resulted.[34] One may express sadness that another interesting concept had been shown to be unviable. Charles Taw, new Works Foreman in the erecting shop, claimed that, given some more money and time, he could have got No. 2299 to work successfully.[35] Yet Tuplin's comment cannot be ignored: it was a 'box of tricks' in which too many untried ideas were mounted on the same chassis.[36]

Paget was little more than an observer on these exploits for he was side-tracked by other things. Up to the 1890s MR trains were not very fast and criticised for poor punctuality. Mathieson as General Manager had done much to improve that situation but Granet wanted still greater improvement.[37] I think we can assume that he saw this not just as a necessary objective for the development of MR operations but also as one that suited his own ambitions. His problem in achieving that objective was that his familiarity with the detail of railway operation was less than perfect. Thus came the need to appoint someone reporting solely to him with all the diverse tendrils of the company's functions gathered under their auspices: a deputy General Manager who would actually be known as the General Superintendent. By this means Granet could represent to the Board as his achievement the day-to-day management of the MR, and also outline his own programme for future development. Paget fitted his needs perfectly. He was not only a consummate conceptual engineer but had views about railway management that offered answers to Granet's specific interests.

Furthermore, he was the Chairman's son. As an introduction to this, I recall an evening many years ago when Carnforth still had platforms on the main line. A group of passengers were awaiting a late running 'up' train and the station manager (was he a station master in those days?) came out onto the platform and explained to the people there gathered what was going to happen. Having done that, his platform inspector said something that I did not hear but to which he replied, 'Oh, I'd better tell Control what I've done.' 'Control' was Paget's most enduring contribution to railway work.

How much the MR Board knew in advance about any discussion between Paget and Granet is not known, though it is not too far-fetched to suggest that Paget senior was aware of his son's ideas. The Board agreed to Granet's proposal and Paget was extracted from Derby to become the new General Superintendent. Paget did have original and foresighted ideas about operational control but I hope I can be excused for suggesting that the fact that he was the Chairman's son was no restraint to Granet's advocacy of his appointment. Enhancing one's career by marrying the boss's daughter is a well-known device; there is nothing different about advocating the promotion of the boss's son.[38]

Paget's proposal was to save money and improve operations by having staff booking-on times and working hours centrally co-ordinated, and then, in 1909, by setting up district controllers for freight operations, a system that was so successful that it was eventually extended throughout the Midland Railway with all operations controlled through a central Control Office at Derby.[39] Thus, the General Superintendent, his office next door to the control room, was able to supervise the working of the whole system. To quote Leech again, he refers to the fact that Paget's habit was to '[conduct] all work by means of long and detailed telephone conversations, often lasting well over an hour ...'[40] A form of this operational control was later extended throughout the LMS and British Railways.

Paget's assumption of his duties as General Superintendent took effect from April 1907, at the time when warnings about the cost of the 2-6-2 must have first been made. The deal was clear; the Midland took on the remaining cost of construction but, because of Paget's occupation with his other duties, Derby would undertake testing and any further developmental work. Now it should be noted that No. 2299 was not completed until January 1909 and Deeley's resignation became effective from August of that year. Deeley did not resign because of the construction of No. 2299;

had that been so he would have gone as soon as the first metal was cut. He may not even have been personally involved with its testing. He announced his decision to resign at the Board meeting at which it was announced that the role of Locomotive Superintendent was to be divided between a Chief Mechanical Engineer and a Chief Motive Power Superintendent. This he was not prepared to accept.[41] The nub of the matter was that the General Superintendent would supervise the running officer who would, as a result, determine the requirements for locomotive and rolling stock construction. If Deeley's objection to this was, at least in part, his objection to being relegated two steps below his former assistant and having what he should build determined by another, then that reaction is perfectly understandable. But it does not necessarily imply a personal animosity towards Paget. And indeed, Deeley's nephew later informed Hamilton Ellis that Deeley's anger was not directed at Paget but 'someone nearer the top'.[42] That someone can only have been Granet, the prime mover in all these goings-on, for central control placed the management of the MR entirely in his hands. A great manager may have to take unwelcome decisions but the test of his success is whether he takes the workforce with him or instead drags it kicking and screaming into line. A system whereby the company's chief executive officer had oversight of all its operations was certainly an appropriate reform but, by pushing it through in the way he did, Granet caused unnecessary disharmony.

That Deeley had not been disposed to resignation even a short time before these contretemps may be assumed from his continued design work. The 4-6-0 proposal had clearly not proceeded beyond an outline drawing. The driving wheels were to be 6 feet, 6½ inches in diameter and the outside low-pressure cylinders 21 inches × 28 inches, with inside high-pressure cylinders at 13 inches × 28 inches. The valves for both sets of cylinders were 8¾ inches in diameter, with the outside valves driven by rocking levers from the inside. The layout is sometimes described as being similar to that of the Churchward four-cylinder engines but that is not entirely correct. Indeed, the outside cylinders placed between the leading driving wheels and the bogie replicated the Crampton layout as developed by his French successors. In this form the inside cylinders were brought forward between the bogie wheels where, in the Deeley proposal, access other than from a pit would have been difficult and further hindered by an access step placed in exactly the wrong place. Given Chapelon's recommendation about valves, those on the low-pressure cylinders ought to have been about 10 inches in diameter. No valve gear type is specified, though I have seen suggestions that, rather than the standard MR Stephenson gear, Walschearts or Stevart gear were considered. Certainly it would have been better to have reversed the proposed layout by having the gear outside, driving the inside valves through the rocking levers.

The boiler looks like a combination of Churchward practice with what was the standard MR approach. It appears to be parallel to and allied with a straight-sided Belpaire firebox but the internal barrel of the boiler tapered about 3½ inches towards the smokebox and the firebox tapered to its rear after the swallowtail shape. The grate, with an area of 30 sq. ft, sloped forward from the backplate. Pressured to 220 lbs/sq. in., the total heating surface was estimated at 1,970 sq. ft. There are a number of apparent drawbacks to the design, of which the steampipe runs appear the most obvious. The outside cylinders are shown receiving steam via a feed pipe that exits the boiler right down at its lowest point, in the water compartment. Although not shown on the diagram, to reach this point the steam pipe, running from the regulator valve in the dome, has to circumnavigate the internal barrel before leaving the boiler. Maintaining the temperature of the live steam would have required very significant lagging of the feed pipe, thereby reducing water capacity. With a superheater and a smokebox regulator valve, the difficulty would have been much reduced.

Despite W. A. Tuplin's comment that it was sad to see Deeley belatedly simulating the Nord's four-cylinder compound layout when it had been shown by Churchward to be wanting[43], the initial drawing, for that is what it can only have been, shows that with development it might have given the compound in Britain a better future. High degree superheat, redraughting the cylinders with larger easier access ports, outside valve gear and large diameter direct steam pipes might very well have made the British railway engineer think twice about dismissing compounding. The proposal dates from 1907, so the suggestion that its development was proscribed because of the policy on train frequency and loading introduced by Paget does not really hold true. It is more likely, I think, that with considerable other work in progress in the period 1907/8, the 4-6-0 was put on one side and, because of Deeley's resignation, never reviewed. Only afterwards, when the new 'small engine' operational policy came into operation, did the 4-6-0 become unnecessary. Running frequent lightly loaded trains, Paget's prescribed policy for the Midland became LMS policy too, until at least 1927, and even after.

There is one other Deeley locomotive that should be noted, one that fits entirely in the characterisation of him as an intellectual and an innovator. As we have noted, the Deeley compound was a success and further batches were built over the period from 1905 to 1909. It does seem that, aware that the compound was hardly regarded as a success anywhere else, he decided to carry out a formal comparison for himself. The result was the 999 class 4-4-0, described by the author referred to earlier[44] as the only Midland design not to have appalling front end design. This had the same boiler as the second batch of compounds, with an extended drumhead smokebox mounted on a separate saddle; originally saturated, they were later fitted with superheaters. 6 foot, 6½ inch driving wheels were driven by 19 inch × 26 inch inside cylinders. What set them apart from the compounds, and indeed all other MR locomotives, was the use of Stevart valve gear. Arguably this negated any comparison between the two types but figures have survived that indicate that, by equalling out load and so on, the coal use per ton mile was lower for the superheated simple than for the saturated compound but that the superheated compound was lower still. This, of course, ruled out the construction of any further 999 class engines though further examples of the sub-Johnson Class 2 types were built, the last in the late 1920s. No doubt this is what so irritated Powell.

Deeley's tinkering with the Stevart gear has become the stuff of myth. Researching this aspect of the design, I find that the accounts of what was done are almost as varied as the number of authors writing them! While he may not be the most popular of commentators, no one can criticise W. A. Tuplin's research. He went back to the primary source for Deeley's patent, the Patent Office records, and declared that it was a modification of Walschearts and not a scissors gear and therefore was not infringed by anything done at Swindon.[45] Moreover, the valve gear fitted to the 999 class was the Stevart gear, in which the expansion link was oscillated by a connection with the crosshead of the other cylinder, not by the Deeley patented modification of Walschearts.[46] The problem with cross valve gears was that they were such a nuisance to set up, and it is much more likely to have been this rather than any prejudice against them that led to the early demise of the 999 class.

With Deeley out of the way the division of the locomotive department's management came into being. James Anderson, already Chief Locomotive

Draughtsman and from 1910 Works Manager, reported, nominally at least, to Henry Fowler, the Chief Mechanical Engineer. To quote Leech again, Fowler, a workshops man with little, if any, experience of locomotive design, was chosen because of 'the desire of the Midland directors to secure an amenable CME ... [and] Paget was passed over...'[47] Design responsibility therefore devolved to Anderson. This gentleman is known to have been opposed to the use of large-diameter, long travel valves and therefore there was little hope that advanced front end design would develop at Derby. This is, therefore, the underlying cause of Powell's criticisms of Midland engines.[48]

Deeley remained unmarried, despite living in a large house in Derby; as related earlier, he busied himself with research in subjects as far away from locomotive engineering as it is possible to find. He died on 19 June 1944 and was buried next to his sister and father in Derby. And what of Paget? He continued as General Superintendent until 1915 when, as mentioned earlier, he joined the Army's Railway Operating Division in France. Again, quoting Leech: 'After the war Paget was too big a man to be acceptable to those who had remained on the Midland during the war ...'[49] and so he went elsewhere. His wife obtained a divorce in 1925 and he subsequently married Florence Butt. He died in 1936, survived by his second wife but without children. Let Clayton have the last word:

> In conclusion it can be said that the Paget locomotive was no freak machine, but an honest endeavour to solve the locomotive problem in a new and simpler way. It ran well and on more than one occasion attained speeds of over 80 mph with its train, proving its capacity to haul a load at high speed; it should be remembered that the driving wheels were only 5'4" in diameter on the tread. As a whole it embodied very many good points and simplicity was throughout its design a characteristic. The simple and straightforward construction of the boiler will be acknowledged while the firebox layout eliminates the usually troublesome copper water space stays and the trouble which is involved in the use of narrow water legs... It seems sad to think that those responsible made no further endeavour to make use of this unique locomotive but as the war of 1914-1918 loomed ahead and all those who might have shown interest in the engine either joined the Railway Operating Division... or retired, so the Paget engine lost all its friends and later was broken up.[50]

Chapter 7

Richard Maunsell: Team Player

A colleague who professes to worship at the gates of Eastleigh Works rather than any place in Wiltshire was mortified when I suggested that Bulleid was 'Gresley without the self-control'. Yet the prevailing idea that the locomotive practice of R. E. L. Maunsell, troubled and uncertain, was swept away by the revolutionary success of Bulleid's Pacific locomotives is a myth that has long passed its sell-by date. For all its initial reputation, it is Bulleid's practice that, certainly in hindsight, can be seen to have been troubled by defects that cost the Southern Railway and BR unnecessary expense in running and rebuilding costs. While certain Maunsell locomotives had shortcomings, these were as much the result of the restraints placed upon him as of any inadequacy on his part. Moreover, his approach was to work co-operatively with other departments; although in 1913 and again in 1923 he knew what he wanted, he did not sweep aside everything and everyone that had gone before. Indeed, that is the very antithesis of what he did.

Richard Maunsell is marked out as being one of the very few Irish-born men to have risen to the highest levels of locomotive engineering on what is sometimes called the mainland, England and its associate nations. He was born on 26 May 1868 in Raheny, County Dublin, a member of a large and wealthy family, with parents who appear to have been supportive and willing to intervene on their children's behalf.[1] His education was not unusual, nor was his reading Law at Trinity College, Dublin. However, he had always wanted to become an engineer and from 1888 he combined his studies with pupillage with Ivatt at Inchicore Works. Graduating in 1891, he came over to England for work experience with Aspinal, then Locomotive Superintendent of the Lancashire & Yorkshire. He met his later wife in Aspinal's household though it was to be some years before he was able to marry her.

On the L&Y Maunsell became Assistant and then District Loco Foreman at Blackpool and Fleetwood. Looking for advancement, he applied for the advertised position of Assistant District Locomotive Superintendent at Jamalpur on the East India Railway. This was a British-owned railway with an important main line from Calcutta (Kolkata) to Delhi, with lines through Jamalpur and Patna and branches to Doltongani and Jabalpur. At this time its locomotive stock was British-built and consisted largely of 2-4-0s and 0-6-0s that would not have been out of place back in Britain. He took up this position in April 1894, later becoming Principal DLS at Jamalpur. The evidence suggests that he pined for his lady friend and was bored with the pace of life on the Indian sub-continent. Hearing that a position was available at Inchicore, he asked for and received release from his contract, returning to Ireland in 1896.

Irish railways were very different to those in Britain. The relative insufficiency of the economy and, among some people, great poverty, indeed the very sparseness of the population, not to forget several periods of civil strife, meant that rail transport was, of a necessity, predicated upon very different foundations to those across the Irish Sea. In the first place mainline railways in Ireland ran on the 5 foot, 3 inch gauge. No one has been able to offer any reasonable explanation for this, for the first railway in Ireland, the Dublin & Kingston, was built to the standard gauge and there were other gauges used, including 6 feet, 2 inches and 5 feet, 2 inches. In a move similar to what happened in England, the British Board of Trade, basing their decision on a curious recommendation from its Chief Inspecting Officer, insisted that 5 feet, 3 inches should become standard and this was established in law by the same Gauge Act that ruled against Brunel's broad gauge.[2] The difference of just 7.5 inches was regrettable; any potential that the wider gauge has for higher speed over the standard gauge has never been exploited. From a purely practical point of view, the most regrettable result was that locomotives from British railways could not be sent across to run in Ireland without regauging. Both the GWR and LNWR and later the LMS had interests in Ireland, which such a facility would have greatly enhanced. As far as the Great Southern & Western was concerned, an added constraint was a maximum axle loading restricted to 16 tons.

Irish passenger trains were too often infrequent and made up of carriages of staggering antiquity, hauled by locomotives that were very old both in conception and construction. Several engineers attempted to right this situation but their efforts were largely frustrated, not just by the socio-economic situation but by a lack of the very commodity they most needed: coal. There were actually plentiful coal measures in Ireland, particularly in the south-west, but they were of very poor quality and unsuitable for locomotive operation. Thus most railway coal had to be imported from across the Irish Sea and its transport around the various railways was a cost factor that weighed heavily on the old companies. I have stressed this detail because Maunsell's time at Inchicore was a crucial learning period for the future.

It was in March 1896 that he moved to the Great Southern & Western Railway, taking up the position of Assistant Locomotive Superintendent and Works Manager at Inchicore. In this position, which he held for no less than fifteen years, he was responsible for the reorganisation of Inchicore works and the replacement of much of the old machinery. E. E. Joynt, Maunsell's Chief Draughtsman, wrote a very detailed description of life and work at Inchicore, which is well worth the study for those interested.[3] Of Maunsell, he said,

> He was splendidly energetic and showed it. He was full of ideas, enterprising, enthusiastic, hard working, and expecting hard work from others. I do not think a happier combination could be found for the management of an engineering establishment than Mr. Coey as chief, and Mr. Maunsell in charge of the shops ... Great works were carried out in which the Mechanical Engineer's department had its share. The size of the boiler shop was doubled, and pneumatic plant and a powerful hydraulic riveter were installed. Modern machines and appliances were added to the machine shop and the smithy.[4]

Robert Coey's most interesting innovation was the American wagon top boiler, which was introduced, after a visit to the USA, on the 321 and 333 class 4-4-0s from 1904. This was a development of the haycock firebox, a cylindrical raised steam space above the top of the inside firebox. Extending above the level of the boiler top, it necessitated a coned back ring to make a flush connection. This provided additional steam space at the hottest part of the boiler and was beneficial to boiler efficiency. Several GSWR engines were built new or rebuilt with this boiler but most were subsequently removed, and it was to be many years before something similar returned to Ireland. Coey experimented with superheating and also introduced 4-6-0 (1905) and 2-6-0 (1907) types, mainly for freight, though the 4-6-0 was not overly successful and did not last very long in service. Coey suffered from health problems, forcing him to resign early in 1911. Maunsell succeeded him and E. A. Watson from Swindon was appointed by the Board to become Assistant Works Manager.

The evidence is that Maunsell and Watson did not get on, maybe because the latter was an Irishman from a very different part of the country, Clones, a small town in western County Monaghan, right on the border with the northern Protestant area. We cannot know how Maunsell regarded Irish nationalism but Watson is known to have been opposed to it and not afraid to say so. The oft-repeated comment by Maunsell about Watson's Swindon ducks and geese may not therefore be the whole story. Watson's training had been with the American Loco Company (ALCO) in its design offices at Schenectady and then with the Pennsylvania Railroad at Altoona. His recruitment by Swindon almost certainly arose from Churchward's wish to have closely available first-hand experience of American railways. Despite this, in the end Swindon was probably glad to get rid of him.[5] Maunsell's confidantes at Inchicore were George V. Hutchinson, appointed his chief assistant, and E. E. Joynt, Chief Draughtsman. Both had seen long service at Inchicore, Hutchinson, since 1904, Joynt even longer.

Whatever he thought of Watson the man, Maunsell did not ignore his ideas, neither in the short nor long term; indeed, Watson's influence on Maunsell's work was profound. It was first evident in the only GS&W locomotive that he completed. This was the superheated 4-4-0 No. 341, named *Sir William Goulding* and delivered to traffic in 1913. The original design had been due to Coey but Maunsell redraughted it with a Belpaire boiler with a heating surface of 1,856 sq. ft and a grate area of 24.9 sq. ft. The 18 inch × 26 inch cylinders had 9 inch piston valves. Fairly obviously, the Belpaire firebox owed at least something to Watson, although Coey's wagon top boilers may well have been similarly influential. The detail design work was done by Hutchinson and Joynt, the superheater in particular being due to Hutchinson. On these bare facts we can assume a powerful and reasonably successful locomotive. Sadly, there are no records of its work that I have been able to locate and, since it was not multiplied (the batch order was cancelled by Watson), we cannot now know what it could do. It was withdrawn in 1928 when the boiler required renewal.

We have mentioned in earlier chapters the bitter rivalry that existed between the London, Chatham & Dover Railway and the South Eastern, which was finally resolved by the amalgamation in 1899 of their operations. Henceforth their activities were administered through the South Eastern & Chatham Operating Committee (SE&C). The first Locomotive Superintendent was Harry Wainwright, previously Carriage and Wagon Superintendent at Ashford. Wainwright was the wrong choice for Locomotive Superintendent both from the point of locomotive design experience and as an administrator. There are differing accounts of his input to the engines described as 'by Wainwright...' but it is sufficient to say that the overall detailed design work was done by Robert Surtees, formerly Chief Draughtsman of the LCDR. Such an arrangement was not unknown elsewhere and could work successfully but Wainwright was a poor administrator who allowed subordinates to get out of control and was unable to withstand the pressure of a Board interested in cutting costs with as little replacement investment as possible. Because of the near-bankruptcy of the two companies in the 1890s, their track, particularly the LCDR north Kent lines, was not suitable for the larger heavy locomotives that the growing traffic demanded. The breaking point came over the directors' wish to close the LCDR Longhedge works without proper compensatory enlargement at Ashford. The consequential crisis was laid at Wainwright's door and he was asked to resign.[6]

It is not unfair, I think, to suggest that Maunsell was happy at Inchicore and would have been prepared to stay there longer but for its limited opportunity for developmental work and indeed for advancement in the profession. So when the SE&C expressed an interest in engaging his services at a much improved salary, it was an opportunity not to be missed. And it was to be the making of him. The Committee Minutes justify the high salary offered with the words: 'Had everything been in satisfactory order it might have been desirable to appoint a younger man at a lower salary. [However] It has been necessary to approach one who has sufficient experience in reorganization.'[7] So, in December 1913, Richard Maunsell, foty-five years old, described as being 'mercurial and a hustler',[8] having 'an explosive temperament'[9] and being a man who got things done, moved to Ashford as CME of the SE&C Operating Committee. Undoubtedly it was this reputation as a 'fixer' that was most instrumental in his getting the job. Knowing about his reorganisation and upgrading of Inchicore Works, the SE&C would have seen him as the ideal man to deal with their own workshop crisis.

The immediate necessity was to borrow locomotives from other railways to fill the gap in available motive power. These consisted of Great Northern 2-4-0s and Hull & Barnsley 0-6-0s, the latter with Mathew Stirling's domeless boilers, running in parallel with the locally built versions designed by his uncle, James. It was at this point that Maunsell made several first class decisions and one extremely bad one. On the drawing board when he moved in was a much amended design for a new 4-4-0 express passenger engine, the L class, a lineal descendant of the Wainwright/Surtees D and E classes. Maunsell was not impressed with the calibre of the staff that he found at Ashford and went outside to find more suitable assistants. In the meantime the drawings of the L class were sent over to Hutchinson at Inchicore for his comments. Hutchinson recommended the adoption of the Inchicore smokebox, a deeper firebox and shortened valve travel with smaller lap. The alterations to the valves were a seriously retrograde step and Maunsell's acceptance of this recommendation is inexplicable. The original L class was never as free running as the later D and E long travel 4-4-0 rebuilds or the L1 class.

This incident suggests that Maunsell was saved by Watson from a terrible mistake. Hutchinson had collaborated closely with Maunsell at Inchicore; the Maunsell superheater, later to become a standard fitting on the Southern Railway, was a design to which Hutchinson made a large input. Maunsell wanted his old PA to move to Ashford but Watson refused to let him go, a decision that in the long term was to Maunsell's undoubted advantage for he now drew most of his new staff from Swindon. As Assistant CME came George Pearson, Churchward's boiler specialist. Surtees remained Chief Draughtsman for a few months until his retirement in 1914 when James Clayton, brought in at the same time as Pearson, took over the position. Clayton we have already met as Paget's draughtsman in the design of his ill-fated sleeve valve 2-6-2. The new Leading Carriage & Wagon draughtsman was Lionel Lynes, also from Swindon. The new Works Manager at Ashford was C. J. Hicks, who Watson had been prepared to let go from Inchicore. A junior recruit, at least at this time, was Harold Holcroft, who had contributed a good deal to Swindon's locomotive development.[10] These assistants were carefully selected and any development they, or indeed others, suggested, Maunsell would examine and those he approved he would adopt, under his name and responsibility.

If Maunsell lacked any superior expertise then it was more than compensated for by the appointment of this high calibre team. There can be no argument that such an arrangement has every advantage and few drawbacks. With a design engineer as significant as, say Churchward, Stanier or even Gresley, single-minded direction from the top may work, but it is significant that both the former drew heavily on talented assistants, Stanier probably as much as Maunsell. This is the very epitome of good design management. We might bemoan the current situation where rolling stock is designed by unnamed committees whose work is more often the assembling of diversely sourced components that take years to bring to operation, but the development of design and production teams as seen on certain of Britain's railways in the early years of the twentieth century was an important industrial progression. Maunsell worked co-operatively with his team and came to rely on them to a large extent. Furthermore, unlike Gresley, he did not intimidate juniors who came up with suggestions.

Holcroft was first put on to preparing plans for the reorganisation, modernisation and extension of loco and carriage works facilities. As far as locomotive development was concerned, Pearson suggested that the lengths of the various SE&C main lines meant that tank engines would be sufficient for passenger work. At first Maunsell was unable to accept this, preferring an outside cylinder 4-4-0.[11] The co-operative efforts of Pearson and Clayton, displaying the evidence to their chief, convinced Maunsell that a tender locomotive was unnecessary and that passenger trains on the SE section could be handled perfectly well by tank engines. The advantages in fuel costs and in operational availability were also clear.[12] As if in confirmation of that, the London, Brighton & South Coast Railway, admittedly with a shorter route, had already decided upon the same policy; Marsh and the younger Billington had built 4-4-2, 4-6-2 and 4-6-4 tanks for exactly that kind of work. Clayton came up with a passenger tank that, to quote Holcroft, 'smacked of Derby' and may indeed have been the 2-6-2T drawn up at Derby immediately before his departure.[13]

Holcroft worked side by side with Clayton for many years and may have felt that his own abilities, and perhaps by association those of his ex-Swindon colleague Pearson, were hindered by a senior officer grounded in the hidebound practices of Derby. Clayton apparently liked the limelight and tended to upstage other people; he could not be initiated into anything innovative unless the instruction came from Maunsell himself. Yet Maunsell appreciated him. In 1919 Clayton was offered the position of General Manager of a private locomotive manufacturer. Maunsell almost literally bribed him to stay at Ashford, offering him an improved salary and status that, once he had accepted the position of personal assistant to the CME, placed him as equal to Pearson. Maunsell's interest in retaining Clayton, we are told, was because he relied on him in matters of detail design.[14] It is never explicitly stated but I think there must have been some abrasion between the Swindon men and Clayton. Whether that is true or not, the reader should bear in mind that, while a good deal of Holcroft's criticism was justified, he was not above pushing his own reputation.

Going back to the early work on the express tank engine, one can well imagine the reactions of Pearson and co. to Clayton's 'Derby tank'. Their alternative recommendation that the design be derived from Swindon practice was accepted; this is interesting because Clayton tended at first to see valve design from Derby's backward stance but he was open-minded and became a convert to modern valve events during the First World War. At that time there was talk about the railways being nationalised at the war's end, and the Association of Railway Locomotive Engineers (ARLE) was tasked with the design of standard locomotives for use throughout the country. There was very little firm agreement between any of the engineers involved but Churchward's views on valve events prevailed. Clayton, involved with the discussion, understood what Churchward was saying and became a strong supporter of large-diameter, long travel valves.[15]

Maunsell's drawing office actually produced five proposals for standard classes, set before the Board late in the summer of 1915. The proposals were for a 2-6-4 express passenger tank (class K), a heavy goods 2-6-0 tender engine (class N), a 4-4-0T for secondary passenger work (class S), a 2-6-2T for suburban and branch line trains (class U) and an 0-6-2T for shunting and yard work (Class V).[16] The crucial point about these proposals is that classes K, N and S were to have the same boiler (with a shortened barrel on class S), cylinders and valve gear. The superheated Class C (0-6-0) boiler was nominated for the remaining types, though I think it is highly unlikely that this would have happened had they actually been built. Inevitably, the taper Belpaire boiler would have figured in the designs. This tends to be confirmed by the existence of a diagram for a 2-8-0 shunting tank authorised in 1919 but never built, which shows just that type of boiler.[17]

Six class K 2-6-4Ts were authorised, as were ten N class 2-6-0s. The exigencies of the war meant that only a single example of each was first built, with both completed in 1917. The Midland cab, outside valve gear and what appeared to be a domed regulator tended to hide their GWR inheritance but it was real enough. Despite the claims of GWR diehards, the change to outside valve gear was right; the demands of accessibility for servicing left no alternative. Sadly, Swindon never really saw the sense of this change. The dome was in fact the top feed apparatus, an ugly device that quite spoilt the appearance of all Maunsell's Moguls. Stanier, after an initial contretemps,[18] did it much better. Top feed actually originated long before this, in Germany in the 1860s; placing the clacks on either side of the safety valve became standard on the GWR from about 1911. Two of the Brighton K class 2-6-0s had top feed, the clacks mounted on a manhole on the first ring of the boiler. Later on, No. 339 was fitted with a top feed dome reminiscent of the German original. Billington later used top feed on the B4X, B2X, C2X and C3 classes.[19, 20] However, this was not its first use in Britain; James Tyrrel had adopted top feed for M&SWJ 4-4-0s Nos 4 and 31, delivered from North British in 1914, again deploying a version of the original German layout combined with Ross safety valves. The use of top feed by Maunsell obviously originated with his Swindon assistants but the Ashford design was derived from the Brighton layout, itself almost certainly inspired by Tyrrel's engines.

Constraints arising partly from the requirements of the war meant that further N class 2-6-0s were not built until 1920 and No. 790 remained the sole 2-6-4T until 1925. Immediately after the war the most immediate need was for express engines for the north Kent boat train services; with the limited strength of the bridges on this route, this could only mean retaining the 4-4-0, and Maunsell delegated the task of developing an improved engine to Clayton. Here again, Clayton's association with Churchward manifested itself in E and D classes rebuilt with large diameter (10 inch), long travel piston valves and with superheaters derived from that used on the N class boilers. The resulting locomotives were superb performers, able to take 300 tons on fast schedules requiring 70 mph running. Holcroft described their riding as 'very lively', which was not a bad feature.[21]

At this time Maunsell was more immediately connected with long-term development of his basic two cylinder 2-6-4T/2-6-0 designs. Into this interesting study the Railways Act came as an intervention that might have blocked everything there and then. It can be argued, with strength in the case of the southern railways, that the actual Grouping arrangement was faulty. The long-distance routes of the LSWR to Southampton and Weymouth and to Exeter and Plymouth had very little similarity to the demands of its own suburban services or to those of the SECR or the LBSCR. It would have made more sense for the Chatham and Brighton companies to have amalgamated with the Great Eastern and taken over the suburban services of the South Western, with its long-distance routes being assimilated into the Great Western. As it was, the motive power demands of the new Southern Railway represented a polarisation that was not replicated on the other three amalgamated companies.

A further complication was electrification, brought into operation by both the Brighton and LSWR and which the new company was determined to extend, particularly after Herbert Walker became sole General Manager of the new Southern Railway in 1924. It should be noted that on the SECR powers for electrification had been acquired as early as 1903 but were never actioned due to an unwillingness or inability to fund the changeover.[22] The SECR suburban traffic was unpopular; it used elderly rolling stock, and had a reputation for running unpunctual and overcrowded trains. Electrification was one answer, though by no means the only one, to that problem. In 1913 a Report commissioned from a Newcastle firm of consulting engineers suggested that the SECR could electrify its lines on a 1,500V DC system. Again, nothing was done until after the war, when Alfred Raworth was appointed electrical engineer. Undertaking wide scale research, including in the USA, Raworth put up to the SECR Board a three stage electrification programme deploying an innovative supply system. This formed the basis of an application for government funding under the 1920 Trades Facilities Act. However, the Board of the three Grouped companies was opposed to Raworth's scheme and decided instead to electrify the SEC lines on the LSWR system, which now became standard. Raworth however was retained as Head of Traction, from 1925 as Electrical Engineer for New Works, and as Chief Electrical Officer from 1938. What contribution, if any, Maunsell made to the original Raworth proposals is not recorded but it will be seen immediately that as soon as he had been appointed CME of the SR, with its commitment to electrification and an enterprising electrical engineer in office, all the ingredients were present for a mighty personality clash between two men essentially engaged in much the same job.

Maunsell's appointment as CME of the SR appears to have been basically automatic. The LSWR's Urie was, in 1923, nearly sixty-nine years of age; it is claimed that he was actually offered the post but declined it.[23] Billington was younger than Maunsell but his senior in terms of service, having been confirmed in office in 1912. He had also put into service more locomotives, including the 4-6-4 express tanks and the K class Mogul. To this writer he seems the obvious candidate for the job and this tends to be confirmed by Holcroft's assertion that he was 'bought off' by the new Board.[24] On the other hand, the researcher might conclude that the Brighton was not held in very high esteem by the new directorship and, given Billington's expressed preference for steam power,[25] would have been seen as an obstacle to the Board's plans, one which it sought to eliminate.

Raworth's personality is also central to SR politics. Sir John Elliott described him as a 'most ruthless professional' with an 'acid' approach to other officers[26] but who got on well with Maunsell. Clearly Raworth was not going to be an easy colleague for anyone and it was certainly to the Southern's advantage that it was Maunsell, the mediator, with whom he had to work rather than a man determined upon his own ideas. It is instrumental to this argument that Elliott goes on to say that Raworth could not stand Bulleid, and who can wonder at it?[27] Maunsell co-operated fully with Raworth and Herbert Jones, another SECR man, the engineer responsible for electrification, despite obvious 'rivalry' between the needs of steam and electric. To this matter I will return later.

The new CME's staff were essentially SECR men, not surprisingly. Clayton, Pearson, Holcroft: the posts of Deputy Chief Engineer, Chief Operating and Locomotive Running superintendents, to say nothing of Raworth, all came from the SECR so that it was the influence of Ashford that predominated even if that was not obvious then or later. At the Grouping the CME's office was established at Waterloo, perhaps to overcome any impression of 'favouritism' by concentrating it at one of the old works centres. It can be argued that this was a mistake; neither Ashford nor Eastleigh were very far from Waterloo. Unlike the LMS or LNER, getting the CME into London for meetings called for no special arrangements and it would have been better to have settled on Eastleigh, which had been designated the principle Loco and Carriage workshops. This too might have dealt with the opposition to

Maunsell's innovations that seemed to emanate from that place. Finlayson, Eastleigh's Chief Draughtsman, appears to have been the focal point for this dissent.[28]

The old LSWR had recovered from the difficulties caused by Drummond's inability to produce a really satisfactory 4-6-0. The fact is, however, that the steaming of the Urie H15/N15/S15 classes, though satisfactory for the use to which the South Western put them, was in reality poor by SEC standards. The valves were old-fashioned short travel devices; the superheater actually obstructed steam flow and required an involved cleaning process. Finlayson must carry a degree of responsibility for these defects because his opposition to long travel valves and other innovations was felt well into the Southern period. The question inevitably arises as to why, when the need arose for further 4-6-0s for the long distance South Western routes, Maunsell did not put his team on to a completely new class of engine. A detailed evaluation of SR steam stock ordered by Maunsell, undertaken to establish the best engines to retain in service, had shown the mediocrity of many of the types then in service. Sweeping them away and replacing them with new designs appears, to us at least, to have been the obvious way forward.

There can be no doubt that the best locomotives in service on the SR in 1923 were Maunsell's new SECR locomotives, with the Brighton K class their only new rivals. It is well known, and the details need no repeating here, that on 21 August 1927 No. A800, *River Cray*, hauling the 17.00 Charing Cross–Deal Pullman train was derailed at 55 mph at Sevenoaks with the result that thirteen people were killed and many more seriously injured.[29,30,31] Investigation showed that several incidences of Rivers 'rolling' had been recorded and problems had been experienced with their effect on the track, there being at least one broken rail reported. It is a detail well known for more than forty years, though little noticed, that Collett called in his assistant works manager, K. J. Cook, to look at drawings of the River bogie and expressed criticism of their design. That said, it can be argued that the real cause of the accident was not so much the design of the bogie as the condition of the track, in particular the effect of poor drainage. Tests on the LNER showed that on good, well-laid track the Rivers performed without trouble, apart from some lurching on certain crossovers. Though Maunsell had been vindicated and track improvements ordered, it seems to have been the General Manager, Walker, who insisted that the Rivers be converted to tender engines, arguably unnecessarily given certain modifications to the bogie suspension. Overall this episode shows, again, the importance of senior executives regularly exchanging information. The Chief Engineer, Szlumper, formerly of the LSWR, was one of the few senior executives not to get on with Maunsell. This strongly suggests that they communicated only when it was essential to do so. Szlumper suffered a nervous breakdown, said to have been caused by the report of the Sevenoaks accident, but the fundamental responsibility lay with SR funding policy, not with departmental officers. I will return to this point later.

It appears to have been Holcroft who put forward the idea of developing three-cylinder versions of the N and K classes. Maunsell had by now recognised that Holcroft was a consummate locomotive man and paid more and more attention to his advice, in this instance leaving the design work entirely in his hands, without Clayton's involvement. In general the design of the N1 and K1 followed that of the two-cylinder variants but they imposed changes that are worth extended examination. With the two-cylinder types the frame design had been along conventional lines but with these locomotives Holcroft wanted to have the three cylinders in two castings bolted together, similar to Swindon practice. However, he was astute enough to see the drawback to Swindon's American derived arrangement by which the plate frames ended behind the cylinders and forged steel bar extensions were bolted on to carry the combined cylinder and saddle castings and buffer beam. This was always a weakness particularly on locomotives with a leading pony truck where this extension had to be braced with strengthening bars affixed to the smokebox. Instead he devised an arrangement by which a deep cut-out in the frame to take the cylinder castings was bridged with a splice plate bolted to it, fore and aft. It is very interesting to note that these frames gave no trouble, while those on the two-cylinder types suffered badly in later years from cracking and distortion. As late as 1955 it was decided to renew them and in many cases completely new frames or half frames were fitted. The opportunity was also taken to fit new cylinders with outside steam pipes and Standard Class 4 blastpipes.[32] The rebuilt engines originally ran without smoke deflectors and their appearance benefited enormously from the change. Sadly, they had to be refitted.

More significant to the design of the three-cylinder locomotives was the use of Holcroft's conjugated valve gear. He had designed the original version of this while still at Swindon and Churchward had shown an interest, although since Swindon did not build three-cylinder engines it was not taken up there. It was in 1918 that Gresley turned out a three-cylinder 2-8-0 with his own design of conjugated valve gear, which aroused a great deal of interest, not to say controversy, and still does. (See Chapter 8) Already the previous year Holcroft had demonstrated a model of his gear to Maunsell, together with a diagram showing how it could be deployed in a three-cylinder 4-4-0.[33] At that time Maunsell had not been disposed to take the matter any further but the 'discussion' about Gresley's engine precipitated certain exchanges both public and private, in the latter case between Maunsell and Gresley, which it is said were not very equable.[34]

As far as the three-cylinder K1 2-6-4T and the first U1 locomotives were concerned, Holcroft was forced by the position of the driving wheels to locate the mechanism in front of the cylinders rather than behind as originally intended. He avoided the use of extended valve spindles, as used by Gresley, with a rod transmitting the motion of the combination lever assembly to the conjugate mechanism located behind the buffer beam. This had the distinct advantage that the valve timing was unaffected by the effect of heat on the valve spindles and the undesired tensing of the conjugation assembly when the engine was working hard. Although the Holcroft layout was probably superior to Gresley's, Maunsell decided, with the batch production three-cylinder 2-6-0s, to deploy three sets of valve gear, with the originals later rebuilt to conform.

Enough has been written here to suggest that Maunsell sat at the head of a very proficient, even talented team of design engineers. Yet it can be argued that they were never given a real opportunity to show their true merit. The Southern Railway was committed to electrification. Walker's determination, strongly supported by Raworth and Jones, made it the central improving activity undertaken. In celebrating this fact, it should be noted that it had downsides that are often ignored. Large-scale electrification restricted the funds available for other purposes, particularly for track improvements and enhancement of the steam stock. Over the period 1923–31 the SR spent £11.8 million on electrification and 293 route miles were adapted for third rail operation.[35] Over the period 1923–1931, the SR spent disproportionately more on electrification than on upgrading the steam stock. 293 route miles were adapted for third rail operation in this period, although there were a further 1,200 route miles still wholly operated by steam power.[35] Maunsell should have pushed the case for greater expenditure on steam power, making the argument that developing standard classes would have reduced actual expenditure, even in the short term. We are told that he was unwilling to push a 'celebrated' General Manager, which is unfortunate.[36] By the same token, the Chief Engineer's objection to Maunsell's Pacific and 2-6-2 designs arose mainly because his annual budget was insufficient for the major track upgrades that were so necessary. As I have already suggested, I believe that this also exonerates Szlumper from any real responsibility for the poor state of the track on the Tonbridge main line.

The only express 4-6-0 that the SR had was the Urie King Arthur, which, it has already been noted, was not then a very successful engine. For express work Clayton favoured a narrow firebox 4-6-0 with maximum route availability but the limits on expenditure meant that only one such type was ever developed, and its availability was limited. At the outset, unable to build a completely new type, Clayton redesigned the N15 front end, improved the air flow through the ashpan, raised the boiler pressure and replaced the Eastleigh superheater with the Maunsell/Hutchinson type. What now became known as the King Arthur class was a much more successful locomotive but, despite what has been written, it could only be a temporary solution. The design of the only new express engine built by the SR, which became the Lord Nelson 4-6-0 class, was not terribly well handled and the reader might very well ask what went wrong.

The intention was to provide a locomotive able to haul 500 tons at a start-to-stop speed of 55 mph, which required about 1,000 dbhp, and reports of their achieving this are known.[37] Yet despite the most careful attention being given to their design, the Nelsons were a disappointment. On paper their dimensions appear near-perfect; the grate area of 33 sq. ft allied with 2,365 sq. ft heating surface was not that much different to the GWR King boiler, although that had higher boiler pressure. Various reasons for this deficiency have been suggested; Holcroft says they were over cylindered and blames Maunsell[38], others point the finger at Finlayson, while Forge wrote: '…the passages for the exhaust were unnecessarily tortuous, and the engine could never really develop its true potential. Some top link drivers could do wonders with them but a high degree of driving skill was demanded to get the best out of a Nelson …'[39] Clearly the fault did lay at the front end and Bulleid later rebuilt them with Lemaitre multiple jet blastpipes; despite what is often written, this was not a complete solution to the problem, which needed another Swindon man, S. O. Ell, to finally resolve.

What the SR needed, as Clayton had advocated, was a standard high performance 4-6-0 with wide route availability, and the Lord Nelson, with its limited utilisation, was no replacement for the 4-4-0s inherited from the pre-Grouping railways. The Schools class is often described as the Maunsell masterpiece, a two-thirds Nelson that replaced the King Arthurs on certain trains. This, surely, is not necessarily a compliment to the Schools so much as an indication that something better than the King Arthur was necessary. That a 4-4-0 should give a performance superior to a 4-6-0, with all the latter's inherent advantages, is extraordinary. If what was required was a general purpose locomotive, better than a King Arthur but with a greater route availability than the Lord Nelson, then a better proposition would have been to develop the SECR type 2-6-0s as 4-6-0s – not, surely, that difficult or expensive a proposition. The fundamental point really is that further development of the Arthurs and, arguably, of the Nelsons, remained the 'mixture as before'; a better approach would have been to start over again, with something new.

During the mid-1930s Maunsell suffered increasingly severe bouts of illness, which led to his retirement in 1937. Much of the work carried out by his staff during that period represented redevelopment of types already in service and showed no particular advancement on what had gone before. The Lord Nelson debacle and what came after suggests that he was a less than successful locomotive engineer. But I cannot accept that. Sometimes he placed too great a trust in certain individuals but his profound capacity for delegation and for melding together a successful design team was demonstrated no less than three times, in Ireland, on the SEC and then on the SR. Furthermore, he could work amicably with other departments. With only two officers does he seem to have had difficulty, with Szlumper and with Finlayson, and in the latter case promotion out of the way ought to have been the recourse adopted. How the SR Board made the astonishing decision to appoint Bulleid as his successor is something I find it impossible to understand.

Richard Maunsell died on 7 March 1944.

Chapter 8

The Contradictions of Sir Nigel Gresley

My friend Leslie Coombs, asked by me to make an assessment of Gresley, wrote, 'I must have a very thick neck or a [huge] ego ... to criticise someone who is an icon. I am mindful that to express opinions on Gresley's decisions is, in effect, *lèse majesté*. In earlier times I would find himself being rowed to the Tower.'[1] Therefore, let your author be clear from the outset: I regard Sir Nigel Gresley as a very distinguished railway locomotive engineer. I am, however, concerned that, although he designed, or directed the design of, outstanding locomotives and components, it was by a developmental process based more on the *ad hoc* nineteenth-century approach than on the enlightened regimes that developed locomotives with as much availability as could be built into them, and for the long-term future rather than immediate needs.

Created by the Grouping, the LNER was welded together as a unit rather more successfully than the LMS because, though the NER tended to dominate, its first General Manager, Ralph Wedgwood, had the management skill and personal acumen to provide the unifying leadership that its success demanded.[2] The appointment of Gresley as Chief Mechanical Engineer was right on almost every count. The Board's preference, G. J. Robinson (GCR), counted himself out, which was probably as well, as his larger locomotives were hardly the most successful then running. Neither Hill (GER), Chalmers (NBR) nor Heywood (GNoSR) had the necessary experience even if they had been interested in the appointment. But it has to be said that, on the evidence, Gresley might not have been chosen had Raven (NER) actually been interested in the job. Though he was only three years younger than Robinson (1856/1859), unlike him he continued at the forefront of locomotive design for some years. Having directed several electrification projects for the NER, his wish was to continue that interest as a director of Metropolitan Vickers. It has been suggested that the resulting choice of Gresley was unfortunate because he did not share Raven's interest in electrification, a contention with which I disagree.[3] Electrification was, and is, very expensive. Whatever else they were, railways were private companies with a remit to provide a return on shareholders' investment. It is clear that many more miles of Britain's railways would have been electrified long before 1939 but for these unavoidable constraints. The LNER was the least financially secure of the four great companies.[4] The NER had been profitable and had good reserves on which to base electrification projects. Yet that situation did not continue into the Grouped railways because the loss-making Great Central became a millstone around the King's Cross neck. The matter of the GCR London Extension ought to have been faced long before BR was forced to do so. In the circumstance of the mid-1920s then, there was no alternative to steam operation by the LNER.

Herbert Nigel Gresley was born on 19 June 1876, the fifth child of the Rector of Netherseale, who was actually a junior member of the Gresley family of Drakelow. Herbert Nigel's cousin, who in due course became the twelfth holder of the title, was actually Sir Nigel Gresley, Bart, so for some years there were two men of this name. Gresley grew up in Derbyshire and was a pupil at Marlborough College before apprenticeship at Crewe and Horwich. By 1904 he was Assistant Superintendent of the Carriage and Wagon Department of the LYR and the following year joined the Great Northern as C&W Superintendent. He was married in 1901 to Ethel Fullagar, a clergyman's daughter, and they had four children. His eldest son, also Nigel, three times married, appears to have achieved very little. It is not easy to be the son of a great man, as many such children can attest. It was Violet, his eldest daughter, born in 1904, who after the death of Mrs Gresley in 1929, became a kind of 'soul mate' to her father, interested in his work and in certain matters his artistic counsellor. Modern generations would not like being called 'Boxy', even by their own family, as Violet was, apparently without protest. Violet's three children are Gresley's living descendants.[5]

The early 1900s were a good time to be entering the British locomotive engineering industry. Several important new 'strands' of design were developing: successful compounding on the MR, big boilered Atlantics and 4-6-0s, piston valves and, most significantly, Churchward's standard designs, batch-built from 1903. Gresley later intimated that his big engines represented a development of the Ivatt principles melded with what Churchward was doing, a claim that the facts hardly justify. Yet, interestingly enough, there is evidence that his early thoughts were to follow the format established by Swindon and to use four cylinders with other Swindon ideas. According to Owen Russell,[6] he actually visited Swindon and was shown round the works by Churchward, Collett and Stanier. What a pity no one thought to photograph that visit; today the mobile phone cameras would have been shooting off at every step of the way! In fact, the first large scale influence upon Gresley appears to have been Ivatt; that, combined with the Great Northern's engine history and the Board's attitude to money, may have had an unfortunate adverse effect on his overall policy.

H. A. Ivatt had taken over from Patrick Stirling as Locomotive Superintendent of the Great Northern from March 1896. The chapter on the Stirlings has shown that, though Patrick's engines were good runners, by the time of his death something more powerful was necessary, but that the parsimony of the Board and the condition of the track made such developments almost impossible. Ivatt is reported to have complained so hard that he actually told the Chairman, 'Had I known the condition of the track I would not have come,'[7] which seems to have done the trick. The civil engineer was given the funding to renew the track and Ivatt was able to get out badly needed 4-4-0 express locomotives. They were obviously different to their predecessors, having domed boilers and cabs with a good deal more cover for the enginemen. In terms of dimensions, however, they were only slightly bigger than the Stirling 4-2-2s, the advantage that they had being, of course, increased adhesion and greater steam space in the boiler. Ivatt rebuilt many of Stirling's engines with domed boilers, including the 2-2-2 and 4-2-2 types, which may have been the encouragement to him to get out his own version. Looking back after 110 years, the observer can only raise his eyebrows at a development that appears so obviously retrograde in nature. There certainly seems to have been a reluctance among certain designers and some boards of directors to acknowledge that, while the bogie single may have been the most attractive machine running on the railways, realism, in the shape of increasing train lengths, weights and speeds, was rendering the type more than obsolete. Ivatt's 4-2-2s lasted less than eighteen years in service.

Ivatt is always associated with the UK's first 4-4-2 Atlantics. Yet I find a disparity in reports of the performance of these engines, not only the 1898 type but the later, bigger version. The original No. 990 has been described as 'an immediate success from the driver's viewpoint ... far less fear of slipping ... steamed admirably'.[8] By contrast, another writer has described them as '… largely an elongation of a Stirling 4-2-2. Outside cylinders were used, the boiler looked long and slender and the engines were never brilliant performers.' Continuing: 'The [GNR] atlantics were heavy on coal…' and rode bad badly because 'of the absence of side control for the trailing axle and by the extremely short rigid wheelbase'.[9] The wheelbase was certainly short; there was only 2 inches between the 6 foot, 8 inch driving wheels. There is an extraordinary story of Ivatt's return from a three-month working tour of the USA in July 1900 to find that No. 990, still the sole GNR 4-4-2, had been kept out of work for most of that time because 'the District Loco Supt. did not hold with coupled wheels for fast passenger work…'.[10] The mind boggles; the man was promoted out of the way but Ivatt would have been justified in dismissing him.

A further ten Atlantics were built in 1900, though it was apparent that with the heavier trains the boilers were inadequate. The question of providing larger boilers, ushered in by the Jones Goods and Dunalastiar classes, was now at the forefront of discussion among engineers and Ivatt, after dallying somewhat pointlessly with a four-cylindered Atlantic, gave his attention to a larger boilered version of the standard engine. These have always been described as the Large Atlantics though, at first, their performance was 'adequate but nothing more',[11] probably because of low degree superheaters and reduced boiler pressure. It was still believed that superheating permitted the use of lower boiler pressure (and, presumably, invoked the hope that boiler costs were thus reduced) when later research showed that the pressure of superheated steam falls between the header and the cylinders.[12] Alterations to the dimensions of the cylinders did not compensate for this decline and the practice actually hampered locomotive efficiency. Ivatt's dislike of superheating is well known; his failure to include reasonably high degree superheating in the Large Atlantics was undoubtedly the Achilles' heel in what was, potentially at least, an outstanding locomotive. The last ten Large Atlantics had Schmidt superheaters and Gresley later fitted thirty-two-element Robinson superheaters as standard.[13] In that form they were hugely improved and gave many memorable – even, in a couple of well-authenticated cases, astonishing – performances.[14, 15]

Ivatt did not enjoy the relationship with the GNR Board that his very high salary suggests he had. Concern about expenditure continued to be a hot topic and ways of reducing cost were constantly in their purview. This was reflected in the Board's wish to try compounding.[16] Reports of the MR and de Glehn compounds had given a brighter view of the concept than that suggested by experiences at Crewe, though the observer is entitled to wonder whether they would have over-ridden their CME's views had they been aware of Churchward's work. As it was, the General Manager's recommendation that Ivatt order a compound Atlantic from the Vulcan Foundry was agreed; he had to comply. H. A. V. Bulleid says that it was a matter of 'prestige' that he should himself design such a machine, by way of providing a comparison.[17] In the event neither showed much, if any, saving on the standard Large Atlantic and in some respects the two-cylinder simple was actually less costly. Almost certainly, with these two locomotives at least, any saving that compounding provided was eaten up by the extra cost of building them. Any assessment of Ivatt's work cannot avoid the conclusion that he was unsure of himself, a traditionalist who was not very happy about new innovations. He is said to have found Gresley 'cocksure and pushing'[18], and given these points, the comment is not surprising: a reaction of a conservative engineer to an enthusiastic newcomer.

In 1911 Gresley was appointed to succeed Ivatt as Locomotive Superintendent of the Great Northern. From the beginning of 1912 his personal assistant was O. V. S. Bulleid, until 1907 Assistant Works Manager at Doncaster, who had spent five years with the French division of Westinghouse and, seeking to return to the GNR, was taken on by Gresley with apparent enthusiasm.[19] The two men got on immensely well; the relationship was a positive one and benefited both. Bulleid remained close to Gresley, going with him to King's Cross when Gresley was appointed CME of the LNER and staying until 1937.

Gresley's first GNR locomotives were noticeably more powerful than Ivatt's engines. Firstly, the original version of the K2 2-6-0 with 20 inch × 26 inch cylinders, 5 foot, 8 inch driving wheels, a boiler pressured to 170 lbs/sq. in. with 1,420 sq. ft heating surface and a 24½ sq. ft grate under a narrow firebox. Outside Walschaerts valve gear with 10 inch diameter piston valves were used. Valve travel at 5⅜ inches was a definite step forward but did not yet reach that of GW locomotives. Although they did very good work it soon became clear that the 4 foot, 8 inch boilers were inadequate and later versions were built with 5 foot, 6 inch boilers and larger Robinson superheaters. The original locomotives were later fitted with these boilers. Gresley's first large freight engine was introduced in 1913, 2-8-0s with boilers in which the superheaters were very large by the standards of the day. Cylinders were 21 inches × 28 inches with the same 10 inch piston valves. A narrow firebox was still favoured; at 27½ sq. ft the grate was about the same as the Churchward 2-8-0, though the boiler heating surface was some 400 sq. ft greater. On the matter of superheating Gresley does appear to have been significantly in advance of thinking on other railways. The 2-8-0s were classified O1 until Thompson relegated them to O3 to allow his rebuild of ROD locomotives to be classified O1. Like the 2-6-0s, they put in admirable service but were heavy on coal consumption[20]; with higher boiler pressure and longer valve travel they would have been even better and probably more cost-effective.

The lull in design work caused by the First World War and the involvement of Doncaster's officers in various kinds of war work did not mean that there was no consideration of future needs. Before going into retirement, Ivatt had told Gresley, 'Don't go to three or four cylinders if two will do the job,'[21] good advice but not to be adhered to, come what may. Increased power meant matching larger boilers to more powerful cylinders and, therefore, to three or four cylinders. In the USA, with its much bigger loading gauge, two-cylinder locomotives could be built to develop the same, and greater, rail horsepower than was possible in Britain; because of that, multi-cylindered engines outside of articulated types were rare in the USA.

The process followed at Doncaster appears faulty and gave misleading results. As far as express passenger work was concerned, Gresley first considered using four cylinders and consequently Large Atlantic No. 279 was rebuilt in 1915 with four 15 inch × 26 inch cylinders and a larger Robinson superheater. Outside Walshearts valve gear was provided, the inside piston valves actuated by rocking levers connected to the outside valves. The consensus view is that the rebuild was under boilered and unlikely therefore to have represented what a four-cylinder engine with adequate dimensions might have achieved.[22] One cannot help but feel that Gresley must have known this and was angling towards the three-cylinder engine anyway. In a paper he read to the Mechanicals in 1925, he made clear his thinking about three-cylinder propulsion.[23] Unfortunately some of the claimed advantages are not wholly convincing and indeed, as has been pointed out[24], in some cases were just repetitions of other points. If there was any advantage of three cylinders over two, it was less hammer blow and, with the gear set at 120°, better starting; neither was outside the capacity of a well-designed four-cylinder locomotive. Remember also that three or four-cylindered locomotives had greater first cost than those with two. Furthermore, an important disadvantage of multi-cylindered locomotives was the need to provide inside valve gear and the restraints that placed on design, access, and cost of construction and maintenance.

However, when the need arose to go beyond two, given the right ratio between the cylinder and valve dimensions and the boiler output, there was no reason why three cylinders should not match the performance of four. Thus, a three-cylinder engine had an advantage in that it demanded less space between the frames, making an accessible layout easier to achieve, with some beneficial effect on first cost. That of course was not the end of the matter, certainly not as far as Gresley saw it. Concerned as he was about cost, there was a definite advantage to be gained in dispensing with the inside valve gear altogether. Thus Gresley's derived, or conjugated, valve gear was created. The facts about this, and a lot of fiction as well, have been written up many times and readers interested therein are referred to the sources referenced in the notes to this chapter. It is sufficient here to cover the main points because they do allow an assessment to be made of the wisdom of this crucially important design decision. Before doing that, the following is a useful overall comment:

> On the drawing board a valve gear arrangement that eliminated the need for inside Stephenson or Walschaerts components must have seemed a gift from the gods of uncomplicated machinery. But there was an alternative way of driving the expansion link and one that proved successful on European railways. This was where the return crank was mounted on the connecting rod pin of a trailing driving wheel. Gresley may have been influenced by the valve gear of Prussian three-cylinder engines. These were located behind the cylinders and not in front, as on the A3s, which was a most unsuitable environment.[25]

In outline, the development of Gresley's gear, worked out on paper during the war, was first incorporated into No. 461, delivered in May 1918, to all intents and purposes a three-cylinder version of the standard (LNER O1) 2-8-0; it had the same boiler with 4 foot, 8 inch driving wheels combined with three 18 inch × 26 inch cylinders, cast in one block, all driving onto the second axle and requiring short connecting rods and steeply inclined cylinders. This last was necessitated by the need to raise the inside drive above the leading axle and was replicated in those outside, which created difficulty in the positioning of the valves. While the outside valves could be got in, just, at an angle inboard of the cylinders and below the footplate run, that to the inside cylinder had to be offset to the side on the central line of its cylinder.[26] There is no definitive answer to the question of why Gresley insisted on a concentrated drive on the second axle when a divided drive would have overcome what was the major criticism of this early form of conjugated gear – that there were too many links and pins. No. 461 did some good work on the Peterborough–London coal traffic, particularly in starting and working at a lower cut off than the two-cylinder class.

As we noted in the last chapter, at this point Holcroft contacted Gresley about this development. Maunsell became involved, as Holcroft's head of department, and met Gresley to discuss the latter's request to be allowed to consult his assistant. Exactly what was said at this meeting has never been revealed but it has been claimed that voices were raised; by whom is not known.[27] In the event Gresley was allowed access to Holcroft, who gave him crucial advice of which Gresley only partly took any account. Holcroft's main suggestion was to put the inside steam chest on a horizontal plane, meaning that its outside compatriots and their adjacent cylinders could also be placed horizontally, allowing the valves to be positioned in a more normal position, above the cylinders. With the three valve boxes on the same plain, a much simplified form of the conjugated gear, with reduced links and pins, could be developed. Holcroft also suggested that the levers of the gear be placed behind the cylinders so that its operation was not affected by the effect of heat change in the valve spindles. An additional advantage of so arranging them was that removal of the valves was easier to achieve.[28, 29]

We have seen in the last chapter that in the SECR three-cylinder locomotives Holcroft had been forced to place the conjugate mechanism behind the buffer beam. Despite this, he connected the levers to rods that transmitted to them the motion of the combination lever assembly. Even though the same kind of constraint caused Gresley to locate the conjugate mechanism of his gear in the same place, he insisted upon connecting the levers to the ends of the valve spindles, a major error that even Gresley's admirers admit was a mistake. F. A. S. Brown declared that it was 'an example of his over-riding of sensible caveats to his ideas'.[30] A possible reason for

Gresley's decision may be that he regarded as undesirable the long link that Holcroft's arrangement made necessary, from the combination lever back, across the face of the cylinder, to the conjugate gear. Additionally, while I have not examined the drawings, it is possible that the vertical cylinder and valve chest cover on Gresley engines interfered with the run of such a connection. All the same, the sheds did not like the arrangement and said so, to no effect.[31]

Going back to Brown's comment, the observer is interested in anything that verifies, or otherwise, this apparent intransigent attitude to advice. A tendency on Gresley's part to arrogance does tend to come over and there is a story that gives an interesting sidelight on this. On one occasion Gresley demanded of Bulleid why his assistants never came up with suggestions. Bulleid said that he didn't know, then added, 'By the way, you remember the draughtsman you agreed to see last week.' 'Of course I do,' replied Gresley. 'The damn fool!'[32] The same book also quotes Gresley on another occasion as telling Bulleid that he was the only assistant he had who would admit to not knowing the answer to something. Both reports are evidence that, while not conclusive, do suggest at the very least that to a lot of his staff, Gresley was unapproachable and that he was not always given straight information about the defects on his engines.

It is interesting to consider just how much of what Gresley did as CME originated in Bulleid's fertile mind. I remain of the view expressed in the last chapter that Bulleid was 'Gresley without the self-control'; an overall examination of the experimental work undertaken by Gresley shows that he never took what I will call a leap in the dark – that is, he did not make the same mistake as Paget and Bulleid and build platforms full of untried innovations. Yet it is also true that he was sometimes slow to take up innovations that tests had shown to be advantageous. The matter of long travel valves and high boiler pressure stand out as the most obvious.

The first locomotive to have the new form of the Gresley gear was a 2-6-0 with 5 foot, 8 inch driving wheels and a massive boiler 6 feet in diameter and 12 feet, 1⅛ inches between tubeplates. Of the total heating surface of 2,308 sq. ft, the superheater accounted for 407 sq. ft and the firebox 182; grate area was 28 sq. ft. With 30,030 lbs tractive effort this was, nominally at least, a very powerful locomotive. It was intended for fast goods work and, often operated at speed, the K3, as it became, gave a good account of itself. However there was a downside in that the flexing of the motion arms led to over travel of the piston valves, with consequent damage to the steam chest covers. Gresley's answer to this problem is astounding: he shortened the valve travel, thus, potentially at least, reducing the efficiency with which steam was used and increasing coal and water consumption. A 2-8-0 with what was now regarded as the standard three-cylinder layout, class O2 was developed from No. 461. The boiler pressure was 180 lbs/sq. in. and the cylinders 18½ inches × 26 inches. Tractive effort was as high as 36,470 lbs. There were eventually 193 K3 class locomotives built up to 1937 and sixty-seven class O2, with the last delivered to traffic in 1934, apart from twenty-five built to replace O4s requisitioned for war work in 1942/3.

Gresley, apparently satisfied that he had got the basic essentials right, turned his attention to the requirements for express passenger trains. This runs in the face of pretty obvious evidence that the derived gear was not working effectively. To quote HAVB,

> Still enraptured with his conjugated valve gear, he too lightly dismissed the snags... And there was always the characteristically, slightly uneven beat, noisily proclaiming that the inside big end was taking more than a third of the duty. Called in as an outside consultant to weigh this evidence Gresley would certainly have voted for a third set of valve gear.[33]

As we shall see, this was only the beginning of a rapture that must have cost the LNER dearly.

Gresley had already had drawn up a four-cylinder Pacific. Having shown that three cylinders could do the job just as well, he turned his attention to developing the three-cylinder derived motion layout for such a locomotive. It is claimed that his inspiration was ALCO No. 50,000, built for the Pennsylvania Railway and developed into the K4 Pacific class, the first of which entered traffic in 1914.[34] In the strict sense I fail to see this; the K4 was a two-cylinder locomotive with bar frames, 27 inch × 28 inch cylinders, 12 inch piston valves with 7 inches' travel, a Belpaire/Wootton firebox and a combustion chamber in the tapered boiler, said to be a significant contribution to its development of 3,200 ihp at 240 rpm.[35] However, the first GNR A1 Pacifics, which Gresley managed to get out in the last year of the company's separate existence, could certainly be described as his basic three-cylinder arrangement merged with a boiler ensemble that owed something, if not to the K4 then to what was standard American practice.

There was no combustion chamber but the firebox was round topped with a wide grate and referenced the characteristic American wagon top boiler design. The boiler was 6 feet, 5 inches internal diameter at the firebox tubeplate end and tapered over its 19 foot length to a smokebox diameter of 5 feet, 9³⁄₁₆ inches. The firebox was 9 feet, 5½ inches long and tapered back from the boiler towards the cab. Gresley resolutely refused to deploy the Belpaire in his engines and thus lost the extra steam space at the hottest part of the engine that this provided. The boiler had a total heating surface of 4,355 sq. ft and was pressed to 180 lbs. This adherence to low boiler pressure is understandable only in the belief that higher pressures caused greater maintenance costs. The cylinders were 20 inches × 26 inches and the valves 8 inches in diameter with 4⁹⁄₁₆ inches' travel. The use of 8 inch valves compared with the 10 inches on the K3 was undoubtedly a handicap to the overall performance and efficiency of the locomotive. Despite this, there is no doubt that the resulting locomotive was a very good performer. To quote just one test run, in September 1922, No. 1471, the second of the brace, took 610 tons from King's Cross to Grantham (105.5 miles) in 122 minutes, including long averages at 70 mph and an average of 45 mph on the 3-mile ascent to Stoke Box.[36] Ten more were built in 1923 and then forty in 1924/5.

At this point it is necessary to pause and to consider the overall approach to locomotive production on the newly formed LNER. Over the years I have written several times about Gresley's unwillingness to entertain the kind of comprehensive standardisation that was practised at Swindon and later by Stanier on the LMS. In one piece I suggested that he was following the line established by the Great Northern's Chairman, Sir Frederick Banbury. In the debate in the House of Commons of the Railways Act, which established Grouping, in 1921, Banbury declared that locomotives suitable for running in one part of the country could not operate anywhere else![37] Taking into account the service life of locomotives such as the Stanier 8F, the Prussian P8 4-6-0 and the DR Class 52 2-10-0, the utter nonsense of this claim is made clear. However, Banbury was not an engineer and moreover had a reputation as a 'character', who may have just been shooting his mouth off in the way that far too many MPs do. That is one view; another relevant question is to ask whether he had been given this information, officially or otherwise, by someone at Doncaster. In other words, did it represent Gresley's thinking? In the straightforward sense in which Banbury used it, I think not. But that it represented an aspect of his opposition to standardisation, I am under no doubt. There is a report of Gresley saying that 'to standardize is to stagnate'.[38] No source for this quote is given but that it does represent his thinking is clear indirectly from the number of new locomotive types introduced between 1924 and 1941, and from Bulleid's expressed view, which was identical. It has been suggested that lack of funding for the locomotive department was the actual reason why a Churchward or Stanier style of standardization was not adopted. This is not born out by the facts.

The locomotive fleets of the major constituent railways represented, as a percentage of the LNER total, 29 per cent from the NER, 18.4 per cent from the GCR, 18.3 per cent from the GNR, 18.1 per cent from the GER, 14.6 per cent from the NBR and just 1.6 per cent from the GNSR.[39] Most of these companies had orders for new locomotives and rolling stock that could not be cancelled, and thus more were built of the GCR B7 and A5 classes, Great Eastern D16 and J68 types, and the NER J27 and B16. Perhaps only the Raven B16 provided anything more than a continuation of the status quo. None of them offered a real prospect of top quality performance ten years hence, the provision of which was the policy that needed now to be adopted. The situation is not analogous with what faced BR in 1948, for at that time the steam locomotive stock of the four pre-Nationalisation companies contained several types that, until replaced by alternative forms of traction, were suitable or, given fairly straightforward modification, perfectly adequate for utilisation on improved high performance services. The case for a new system of standardisation was completely unjustified. In the circumstances of 1923, with an inheritance of locomotives that did not have potential for long-term advanced performance, the case for standardisation was blatantly obvious.

Bonavia states that the financial position of LNER restricted what Gresley could do.[40] That is not untrue but analysis of the figures gives a rather different picture to the one intended. Before going on, I should make it clear that a strict comparison of expenditure on locomotives by the GWR and LNER is rendered impossible because of different accounting procedures. As an example, in its Annual Reports in the first years of the last century, the GWR refers to the costs of new locomotives but also to the application made for capital investment in them. From this it is clear that the funding of new stock was made from both Capital and Revenue accounts.[41] Short of physically totting up the total costs of each new engine or rebuild, a next to impossible task, an exact figure for expenditure on this specific item is not possible.

It is similar for the LNER in the 1920s, where overall figures that include maintenance and 'renewal' are given together with a figure specifically for new locomotives. The exact meaning of the word 'renewal' is not given but can clearly cover anything from a new engine to a rebuild.[42] A further complication, though it should be relatively easy, is the factor of inflation. There is no difficulty in using the Bank of England's online calculator to work out that at 1924 prices, the GWR spent, in 1900, £4,326,604 overall on locomotive department expenses, though the request by the Board for capital expenditure was, again at the 1924 figure, £101,086. These figures compare strikingly with what the LNER declared in 1924, £4,076,579 overall and £741,119 specifically for locomotives.

A difficulty occurs if we move forward and compare the expenditure by the GWR in the years 1900 to 1910 with that of the LNER from 1924 onwards. The appalling monetary policy imposed by the Bank of England on the governments of the day was the essential cause of a deflationary spiral that affected the British economy from 1920, almost without break until 1934. Thus the 1926 figure of £3,483,742 spent overall is actually higher by about £17,500 when adjusted to the 1924 value. Despite what might be thought, deflation, nor for that matter very low inflation, does not make prices cheaper; it makes investment difficult and inhibits growth. It would be very interesting if a historical accountant could attempt to unravel these figures or, indeed, the railway company's accounts overall, for they might reveal that a lot of what we have been led to believe is the stuff of myth.

Given, then, the following figures from the LNER's accounts for expenditure specifically on new locomotives – 1924: £741,119, 1925: £341,116, 1926: £62,855, 1927: £429,164, 1928: 626,791 – the conclusion cannot be avoided that Gresley did have sufficient funds to undertake a system of advanced standardisation. That he did not use his budget for this purpose, justifying that with the nonsense about stagnation, is a serious flaw in his overall reputation. There is no question that Gresley was right to believe that his A1 Pacific represented a viable long-term future express passenger locomotive for the Grouped railway, even though such a consideration ignored the Raven Pacific of which, at that time, nothing was known. But there was no strategic assessment of the overall needs of all types of traffic, new building went on piecemeal and unsystematically, as it always had. Twenty years later, during wartime no less, Thompson set out a plan that envisaged building two Pacific classes, one for express passenger services, one for heavy mixed traffic; a 4-6-0 and a 2-6-0 for general work; a 2-8-0 freight engine; a mixed traffic tank and two types of shunting engine.[43] With the same boiler and cylinders used on the two Pacifics, the 2-8-0 and 4-6-0 sharing the same boiler and cylinders, and the mixed traffic 2-6-0 devolved into a 2-6-2 or 2-6-4 version, a realistic and viable system results. The only potential difficulty is designing with an eye for future intermediate to long-term needs, but it can be done without stagnation, as was shown by Churchward, Stanier and in Europe, in Germany in particular.

The GNR 4-6-2, delivered in a blaze of publicity in April 1922 and carrying the name *Great Northern*, excited railway engineers and enthusiasts alike. In size it was much bigger than anything that had previously run on the GNR and, apart from *The Great Bear*, was the biggest express passenger locomotive then built. The following month the NER published drawings and detailed figures of its own Pacific, designed by Vincent Raven but not actually delivered to service until November, immediately before the Grouping took effect. Under the classification system adapted by the LNER from that of the NER, they were known as classes A1 and A2. I have always thought that this was an ideal system of classifying locomotives, especially as it allows sub-classification of rebuilds as, say, A2/1. If the system had a fault it was that tank engines should have started at A50, whereas the Pacifics ran from A1, 2, 3, and 4, which were tender engines, but then continued as A5, 6 and 7, which were tanks. Thompson really spoilt it all by reclassifying the surviving A1s as A10 and his own engines as A1 and A2, which Peppercorn continued. I suppose he did not like the idea of his brave new engine being designated A10, especially as the GWR had a Castle that carried the number 100A1.

The original Gresley A1 and Raven Pacifics have always been seen as being directly in competition and some observers, particularly certain individuals who should have known better, have dismissed the Raven engine as outclassed from the start. This is not entirely true. They came about because there was a requirement for something more powerful and quicker starting than the Z class 4-4-2s.[44] Like the Zs, they had three 19 inch × 26 inch cylinders cast in monobloc form, 6 foot, 8 inch driving wheels and inside Stephenson valve gear. The total heating surface was 2,874 sq. ft, of which 510 sq. ft was represented by the Schmidt superheater. The wide firebox had a grate area of 41½ sq. ft. On account of its parallel flush top the boiler appeared longer than it actually was; a combustion chamber 2½ feet long was fitted ahead of the firebox and the front tube plate was recessed into the boiler. This gave an internal barrel length of 21 feet. Critics have said that, because it was a 'long drawn out version' of the class Z rather than a completely new design, the A2 was somehow less likely to be successful.[45] Yet the boiler, under test, produced all the steam required of it and maintained better temperature and pressure level than that of the A1.[46] The figures for coal consumption appear to be rather different, 58.7 lbs against 52.6 lb/mile, but this has to be ameliorated to the loads behind the engine and the prevailing weather conditions. Moreover, the later Hughes 4-6-0s with their long travel valves burnt 50.2 lbs/mile[47] so both Pacific types tended to be what Tuplin described, in another context, as 'miners' friends'. At that stage, 1923, providing the A2 with a redesigned front end might have actually made it superior to the Gresley A1.

It is not necessary to repeat again the events that, at long last, persuaded Gresley that he was wrong to oppose the use of long travel valves and high boiler pressure. Taking first a half step forward with No. 4477 *Gay Crusader*, he next had No. 2555 *Centenary* refitted with valves in which the travel was extended to 5¾ inches and the lap to 1⅝ inches. This in itself transformed the engine; the coal use was reduced to 38 lbs per mile – that is to say, a saving of about 20 per cent.[48] The final part of the transformation was the fitting of a boiler with 220 lbs boiler pressure containing a superheater about 15 per cent larger. Thus rebuilt, the A3 class was created, one of the truly great locomotive designs built in Britain. Thirty-two new-build A3s were built between 1928 and 1932 and rebuilding of the original A1s was put in hand. The achievement of No. 2750 *Papyrus* in running at an average speed of 100.6 mph for over 12 miles, from Corby to Tallington, in March 1935 was an extraordinary achievement, the first unassailable 100 mph speed recorded in the British Isles.[49, 50] This was a fitting preliminary to Gresley's development of the streamlined A4 Pacific, an all-time classic.

These historic achievements gave lustre to Gresley's name and that of the LNER. But there is another story. Bonavia says that, while the financial results were good, there was a disparity between Gresley's claims and those made by other LNER officers. Gresley claimed the income was 13s 11d per mile against expenses of 2s 6d. Different figures have also been given, 16s 2d per mile income against 4s 2d expenses. The receipts from the high-speed streamlined trains were actually higher than the average of LNER receipts; during July 1938 the profit on four streamlined trains was about £22,000.[51]

And then, to quote LFEC again,

'Horses for courses' is a most appropriate summary of Gresley's policy ... The most significant example of this overall policy were the locomotives intended for specific routes or trains such as P1 & P2. The former were capable of hauling 1600 ton coal trains and avoided the need to double-head such loads. However, they were before their time. Had there existed high capacity wagons then the trains would not have caused operating difficulties because of their length. Sometimes a train could extend across two signal blocks. From a signalman's and traffic controller's points of view they were unwieldy. Another adverse factor and one that does not seem to have been commented upon to any great extent, was the need on occasions to stop quickly a 1600 ton train of loose-coupled wagons with brakes only on the loco and van. The P2s were intended to handle 500 ton passenger trains between Edinburgh and Aberdeen. The length of their trains presented the operating problem of the need to draw up twice at some stations. The attempt to provide powerful locomotives seemed to have blinded Gresley to the operating difficulties of long trains. Surely he and his design team consulted the traffic and signals departments? If they did put forward their reservations concerning the use of these engines then did Gresley ignore them?[52]

Readers who challenge these arguments about standardisation should look at the timeline (below) of new designs that appeared in the years 1925 to 1941 (the Pacifics of both A1, A3 and A4 classes have been omitted from this list, as have the considerable number of pre-Grouping locomotives built new or rebuilt under Gresley).

1925
2-8+8-2 Garret built by Beyer, Peacock to Gresley requirements. Derived from Robinson design not actioned, 'double' three-cylinder conjugated

drive. Machinery interchangeable with O2 2-8-0. One only built for banking duties.

P1: three-cylinder 2-8-2 heavy freight loco, see above, two only built. A1 type boiler later replaced with A3 boiler. Original cost of these locomotives was £10,000 – £2,000 up on budget estimate.[53]

1926

J39: Two-cylinder 0-6-0 with 5 foot, 2 inch driving wheels, 289 built for goods work.

J38: As J39 with 4 foot, 8 inch driving wheels and originally different boilers. Later fitted with J39 boilers. Thirty-five built.

1927

D49: Three-cylinder 4-4-0 designed at Darlington, for express passenger work, derived motion behind cylinders, other Darlington 'specialties', J39 boiler. Seventy-five built, three different valve gears used.

1928

B17: Three cylinder express passenger 4-6-0 designed by North British to Gresley requirements for lightly loaded routes, divided drive and conjugate gear behind cylinders. Despite claims to contrary, not really superior to B12.[54]

1929

4-6-4 high-pressure compound locomotive with Yarrow water tube boiler; known as the 'Hush Hush', rebuilt in 1936 as conventional three-cylinder locomotive with modified A4 boiler, classified W1. Worked in A4 rosters.

1930

V1: Three-cylinder 2-6-2 mixed traffic tank engine, essentially for suburban passenger work.

1934

P2: Three-cylinder 2-8-2 for express passenger work on Scottish east coast route. Original had rotary cam poppet valves, later engines had Walschearts gear. Six only built, later streamlined in A4 form.

1936
V2: Three-cylinder fast mixed traffic 2-6-2 derived from A3s extensively used on express passenger work. Wheel arrangement allowed use of wide firebox. 184 built and deployed throughout the LNER system.

1937
K4: Three-cylinder 2-6-0 with 5 foot, 2 inch driving wheels for use on lightly loaded and curved main lines, e.g., West Highland Line. K3 cylinders with smaller boiler. Six only built.

1939
V3: V1 with 200 lbs pressure. Many V1s later upgraded to V3.

1941
V4 2-6-2: Three-cylinder 2-6-0 'general purpose' locomotive for use where larger locomotives barred. Two only built, almost certainly because Thompson was against further construction.

During the same period he also proposed a 2-6-4T to replace the B12s on the GE and for the GN suburban services, a three-cylinder 2-8-2T for the Nottingham coal traffic, a three-cylinder 4-6-0 to replace the B17 and K3, a high acceleration 2-6-4T and a 4-8-2 express passenger locomotive. Despite the highly successful V2 class, and the K3 and O2 inherited from the GNR, also batch-built after 1923, I fail to see any systematic plan here other than that which LFEC calls 'horses for courses'. The most astonishing point to observe, however, is the fact that, apart from the J38/39 0-6-0s, all these are three-cylinder locomotives, even the 2-6-2Ts, with some form of derived drive that, in the final analysis, was not operating at maximum benefit to the steam cycle, even when new; the problems were not entirely cured by modification. Even allowing for the fact that, as a general running matter, it could be operated successfully, Thompson was absolutely right to want to drop the 2-1 valve gear and the report by Sir William Stanier and his team, now available in the public domain, leaves no doubt about this.[55] For a man with the undoubted technical talent that he had, Gresley's zealotry for the conjugated valve gear is incomprehensible, unless it was a part of his determination to be seen to be his 'own man'. This was undoubtedly a factor in Gresley's failing to reduce locomotive construction and maintenance costs.[56]

Sir Nigel died of heart failure, brought on by overwork, on 5 April 1941. His death was marked by obituaries that appropriately celebrated his undoubted achievements. History, however, leaves us no option but to temper our own admiration with acknowledgement of factors that were then either unrealised or ignored.

Notes and References

Chapter 1

1. Gooch, Sir Daniel, ed. John Gooch, *The Diaries of Sir Daniel Gooch*. There are three published versions of what is actually a note of his early work and only subsequently a diary; the quoted extracts in this chapter are from the original edition published in 1892.
2. Vaughan, A. H., *Isambard Kingdom Brunel: Engineering Knight Errant*.
    Vaughan, A. H., *The Intemperate Engineer*.
    Vaughan, A. H., *LTC Rolt: Myth-maker*.
3. Gooch, *The Diaries of Sir Daniel Gooch*.
4. Baker, P. H., 'John Viret Gooch', *Back Track*, May 1995.
5. Gooch, *The Diaries of Sir Daniel Gooch*.
6. Ibid.
7. Clarke, Seymore, *Traffic Superintendent's Reports to the GWR Board* (National Archive).
8. Gibbs, G. H., ed. Jack Simmons, *The Birth of the Great Western Railway: Extracts from Gibbs Diary & Correspondence*.
9. Gooch, *The Diaries of Sir Daniel Gooch*.
10. Ibid.
11. Ibid.
12. Ibid.
13. There's an idea for someone!
14. At the same time it is only fair to add that the narrow gauge lines did catch up and eventually surpassed broad gauge locomotive performance, but only because of the inertia that set in on the GW and lasted until the late 1880s.
15. *Guinness Book of Records*.
16. The distinction is important because the cheetah can reach maxima of 75 mph for short-length chases and has a very high rate of acceleration.

17. MacDermot, E. T. and Clinker, C. R., *History of the Great Western Railway* Volume 1.
18. Sam Bee, Fire Fly Trust: verbal information to the author.
19. They never were; they were only drawn up long afterwards.
20. Gooch, *The Diaries of Sir Daniel Gooch*.
21. Ibid.
22. Marshall, J., *The Guinness Book of Rail Facts & Feats*.
23. Gooch, *The Diaries of Sir Daniel Gooch*.
24. Holcroft, H., *Outline of Great Western Locomotive Practice*.
25. Correspondence with the author, December 2015.
26. Gooch, *The Diaries of Sir Daniel Gooch*.
27. Rolt, L. T. C., *Brunel*.
28. Vaughan, A. H., *Isambard Kingdom Brunel: Engineering Knight Errant*.
29. Today the figure of Kw is the 'authorised' measure of power output and 1 British horsepower is the equivalent of 0.7457 Kw.
30. Phillipson, E. A., *Steam Locomotive Design Data and Formulae*.
31. Peck, A. S., *The Great Western at Swindon Works*.
32. Summers, L. A., *Swindon Steam: A New Light on GWR Loco Development*.

Chapter 2

1. Wikipedia article on Crampton.
2. *Grace's Guides*: Quoted from the biography reprinted from the *Engineer* magazine.
3. Lowe, James W., *British Steam Locomotive Builders*.
4. Website of Crampton Tower Museum: www.cramptontower.co.uk.
5. Westwood, J. N., *Locomotive Designers in the Age of Steam*.
6. Sharman, M., *The Crampton Locomotive*. This is the most detailed book on this subject but it does contain several errors, not all of which are the fault of the author.
7. Sharman, *The Crampton Locomotive*.
8. Bradley, D. L., *The Locomotive History of the South Eastern Railway*.
9. Sharman, *The Crampton Locomotive*.
10. Diaries of David Joy. The microfilm copy of the original document held in the Science Museum Library at Imperial College was the source for this statement.
11. Hamilton Ellis, C., *Some Classic Locomotives*.

12. Ibid.

13. Ahrons, E. L., *The British Steam Locomotive 1825–1925*.

14. Phillipson, *Steam Locomotive Design Data and Formulae*.

15. Hamilton Ellis, *Some Classic Locomotives*.

16. Ibid.

17. Sharman, *The Crampton Locomotive*.

18. Hamilton Ellis, *Some Classic Locomotives*.

19. Sometimes quoted as 1852.

20. Sharman, *The Crampton Locomotive*.

21. Crampton, T. R., 'Construction of Locomotive Engines', *Proc.ICivE* 1849.

22. *Grace's Guides*, quoted from the biography reprinted from the *Engineer* magazine.

23. Ibid.

24. A description of Crampton's valve gear will be found in Shields, T. H., *The Evolution of Locomotive Valve Gears*.

25. www.levantineheritage.com/pdf/orc_history.pdf.

26. Sharman, *The Crampton Locomotive*.

27. Hamilton Ellis, C., *Twenty Locomotive Men*.

28. Diaries of David Joy. See note 10.

29. Remember also that before the British slave trade was abolished, the Bristol promoters of the GWR, the members of the Merchant Adventurers' Society, had made a great deal of money from it.

30. Sharman, *The Crampton Locomotive* contains a photograph and diagrams of these locomotives.

31. Ibid.

32. Hamilton Ellis, *Some Classic Locomotives*.

33. Sharman, *The Crampton Locomotive*.

34. Chapelon, A., *Locomotive a Vapeur*.

35. Sharman, *The Crampton Locomotive*.

36. Ibid.

37. Hamilton Ellis, *Some Classic Locomotives*.

38. *La Continent* was actually put back into working order after the First World War and ran for several years before final withdrawal in 1924.

39. Bradley, *The Locomotive History of the South Eastern Railway*.

40. Ibid.

41. Ibid.

42. Sharman, *The Crampton Locomotive*.

43. Bradley, D. L., *The Locomotive History of the London, Chatham & Dover Railway*.
44. Ibid.
45. Ibid.
46. Hamilton Ellis, *Twenty Locomotive Men*.
47. Sharman, *The Crampton Locomotive*.
48. This information the author has extracted from an untitled cutting in an old engineering journal.
49. Anthony, Pierre, 'French Crampton type locomotives', *Locomotive Magazine*, October 1932.
50. This information the author has extracted from an untitled cutting in an old engineering journal.
51. See the chapter on the Stirlings in this book.

Chapter 3

1. Hamilton Ellis, *Twenty Locomotive Men*.
2. See Wikipedia in particular.
3. Peck, *The Great Western at Swindon Works*.
4. MacDermot and Clinker, *History of the Great Western Railway* Vol. 1.
5. Hamilton Ellis, *Twenty Locomotive Men*.
6. *Grace's Guides*, quoted from the biography reprinted from the *Engineer* magazine.
7. Ahrons, E. L., *Locomotive & Train Working in the Latter Part of the 19th Century*. Volume 1 of the series published in book form.
8. Foxwell, E., *Express Trains*. Quoted by Ahrons in reference 7.
9. Lowe, James W., *British Steam Locomotive Builders* and other references.
10. Gibson, J. C., *GWR Locomotive Design, a Critical Survey*.
11. Hamilton Ellis, *Twenty Locomotive Men*.
12. *Dictionary of National Biography* 1912 Supplement.
13. Bradley, *The Locomotive History of the London, Chatham & Dover Railway*.
14. Dow, George, *Great Central*.
15. Holcroft, H., *The Armstrongs of the Great Western* contains a useful chapter on the early vacuum brake.
16. Dow, *Great Central*.
17. Ibid.

18. Hamilton Ellis, *Twenty Locomotive Men.*
19. Ahrons, *Locomotive & Train Working in the Latter Part of the 19th Century* Vol. 1.
20. Foxwell, *Express Trains*, quoted by Ahrons in *Locomotive & Train Working in the Latter Part of the 19th Century* Vol. 1.
21. Ahrons, *Locomotive & Train Working in the Latter Part of the 19th Century*, Vol. 1.
22. Ahrons, E. L., *The British Steam Locomotive 1825-1925.*
23. Private correspondence.
24. Ahrons, *The British Steam Locomotive.*
25. Ahrons, *Locomotive & Train Working in the Latter Part of the 19th Century*, Vol. 1.
26. Dow, *Great Central.*
27. Ibid.
28. Ibid.
29. Hamilton Ellis, *Twenty Locomotive Men.*
30. Rolt, L. T. C., *Red for Danger.*
31. Hamilton Ellis, *Twenty Locomotive Men*
32. Longfellow, H. W., 'The Masque of Pandora', but believed to have been derived from Sophocles: *Quos deus vult perdere, prius dementat.*
33. The current Channel Tunnel follows a different route, separate from Watkin's tunnel.

Chapter 4

1. Information from Hull & Barnsley Railway Stock Fund.
2. *Grace's Guides*, quoted from the biography reprinted from the *Engineer* magazine.
3. Ibid.
4. Summers, *Swindon Steam.*
5. Hamilton Ellis, *Twenty Locomotive Men.*
6. Tyldley, J., 'Who Lived There?', *Back Track*, November 2000.
7. Lowe, James W., *British Steam Locomotive Builders.*
8. *Grace's Guides*, quoted from the biography reprinted from the *Engineer* magazine.
9. Ibid.

10. Hills, R. L. and Patrick, D., *Beyer, Peacock: Locomotive Builders to the World*.

11. Hamilton Ellis, *Some Classic Locomotives*.

12. Hills and Patrick, *Beyer, Peacock*.

13. Leech, K. H. and Body, M. G., The Stirling Singles.

14. Ibid.

15. Ahrons, E. L., *Locomotive & Train Working in the Latter Part of the 19th Century* Volume 3.

16. Quoted in the Steamindex website.

17. Leech and Body, The Stirling Singles.

18. Rolt, L. T. C., *Patrick Stirling's Locomotives*.

19. Churchward, G. J., 'On Large Locomotive Boilers', *Proc.IMechE* 1906.

20. Highet, Campbell, *Scottish Locomotive History*.

21. Hamilton Ellis, *Twenty Locomotive Men*. Hamilton Ellis is quoting Dendy Marshall but the remark has been widely reported.

22. Rolt, *Patrick Stirling's Locomotives*.

23. Bird, G. F. and Christopher, John, *Locomotives of the Great Northern Railway*.

24. Ahrons, *The British Steam Locomotive*.

25. Leech and Body, The Stirling Singles.

26. Notes on Patrick Stirling in the Steamindex website.

27. Leech and Body, The Stirling Singles.

28. Ibid.

29. Ibid.

30. Cox, E. S., *Locomotive Panorama* Volume 1.

31. Nock, O. S., *The Railway Race to the North*. Quoted from the *Engineer* with accompanying logs drawn up by the author.

32. Ahrons, *Locomotive & Train Working in the Latter Part of the 19th Century* Vol. 1.

33. Ahrons, *Locomotive & Train Working in the Latter Part of the 19th Century* Vol. 3.

34. The last such 4-4-0 was not withdrawn until 1962.

35. Improbably but actually pronounced 'Smiley'!

36. Ahrons, *Locomotive & Train Working in the Latter Part of the 19th Century* Vol. 3.

37. Ibid.

38. Bradley, *The Locomotive History of the London, Chatham & Dover Railway*.

39. Ibid.

40. Ahrons, E. L., *Locomotive & Train Working in the Latter Part of the 19th Century* Volume 5.

41. Kidner, R. W., *The South Eastern Railway and the SE & CR.*

42. Middlemass, Tom, *The Scottish 4-4-0.*

43. Hamilton Ellis, C., *Four Main Lines.*

44. Acworth, W. M., quoted in Ahrons, *Locomotive & Train Working in the Latter Part of the 19th Century* Vol. 5.

45. Nock, O. S., *Speed Records on Britain's Railways.*

46. Rous Marten, C., 'Locomotive Practice & Performance', *Railway Magazine,* January 1907.

47. Leech and Body, The Stirling Singles.

48. Ahrons, *Locomotive & Train Working in the Latter Part of the 19th Century* Vol. 1.

49. Nisbet, A. F., 'The Attempt on the Life of James Stirling', *Back Track,* November 2010.

50. Ingram, M. E., Hoole, K., Hinchliffe, B., *History of the Hull & Barnsley Railway* Volume 2, Chapter 9, 'Locomotives' by K. Hoole.

51. Information from Hull & Barnsley Railway Stock Fund.

Chapter 5

1. Hamilton Ellis, C., *The South Western Railway: Its Mechanical History and Background, 1838–1922.*

2. Forge, E. L., 'Eastleigh and Locomotive Design' Part 2, *Railway World,* November 1983.

3. Much of this detail comes from the reproduction in *Grace's Guides* of biographies that appeared originally in the *Engineer.*

4. Hamilton Ellis, *Twenty Locomotive Men.*

5. Chaksfield, J. E., *The Drummond Brothers: A Scottish Duo.*

6. Ibid.

7. Ibid.

8. Much of this detail comes from the reproduction in *Grace's Guides* of biographies that appeared originally in the *Engineer.*

9. Rolt, *Red for Danger.*

10. Middlemass, *The Scottish 4-4-0.*

11. Highet, *Scottish Locomotive History.*

12. Chaksfield, *The Drummond Brothers.*

13. British finance was very involved in Australia and indeed other dominions as well. A Crown Agent was maintained to liaise between railway companies and British manufacturers.

14. Lowe, *British Steam Locomotive Builders*.

15. Ahrons, *Locomotive & Train Working in the Latter Part of the 19th Century* Vol. 3.

16. Nock, *The Railway Race to the North*.

17. Ahrons, *The British Steam Locomotive*.

18. Atkins, C. P., *The Scottish 4-6-0 Classes*.

19. Cormack, J. R. H. and Stevenson, J. L., *Highland Railway Locomotives*.

20. McKillop, N. (writing as Torem Beg), 'Highland Interlude', *Trains Illustrated*, August 1957.

21. Cormack and Stevenson, *Highland Railway Locomotives*.

22. Much of this detail comes from the reproduction in *Grace's Guides* of biographies that appeared originally in the *Engineer*.

23. Middlemass, *The Scottish 4-4-0*.

24. Highet, Campbell, *The Glasgow & South Western Railway*.

25. Hamilton Ellis, *Twenty Locomotive Men*.

26. Drummond, D., 'Particulars of the most recent parts of the London & South Western Railway Company's Engines', *Proc.ICivE* 1897/8.

27. Chaksfield, *The Drummond Brothers*.

28. The Holmes 4-4-0s of the NBR were derived from and essentially Drummond engines in concept.

29. Nock, *The Railway Race to the North*.

30. Ibid.

31. Middlemass, *The Scottish 4-4-0*.

32. By the same token, the GSWR 0-6-0T preserved in Glasgow is not a Drummond engine but clearly the work of the manufacturer, North British.

33. See amongst other references *Railway World*, July 1966.

34. Cormack and Stevenson, *Highland Railway Locomotives*.

35. Ibid.

36. Ahrons, E. L., *Locomotive & Train Working in the Latter Part of the 19th Century* Volume 4.

37. Hamilton Ellis, *The South Western Railway*.

38. Chaksfield, *The Drummond Brothers: A Scottish Duo*.

39. Atkins, *The Scottish 4-6-0 Classes*.

Chapter 6

1. Atkins, C. P., 'Richard Mountford Deeley: Author & Polymath', *Midland Record Society Journal*, 2004.
2. Deeley, R. M., *A Genealogical History of Montfort-Sur-Risle and Deeley of Halesown.*
3. Atkins, 'Richard Mountford Deeley'.
4. Ibid.
5. Powell, A. J. (writing as '45671'), 'Living with LM Locomotives', *Trains Illustrated*, November 1957.
6. Summers, A. W., *Engines Good and Bad.*
7. Johnson, J. and Long, R. A., *British Railways Engineering 1948–1980.*
8. Radford, J. B., *Derby Works and Midland Locomotives.*
9. Leech, K. H., 'Midland Railway 8-cylinder 2-6-2 No. 2299', *Railway Gazette*, 2 November 1945.
10. Ibid.
11. Radford, *Derby Works and Midland Locomotives.*
12. Leech, 'Midland Railway 8-cylinder 2-6-2 No 2299'.
13. Ibid.
14. Hamilton Ellis, C., *The Midland Railway.*
15. *Locomotive Magazine*, 5 September 1903.
16. See particularly Ahrons, E. L., *Locomotive & Train Working in the Latter part of the 19th Century* Volume 2.
17. Aoki, Eiichi, *Japanese Railway History: Dawn of Japanese Railways* (accessed via the internet).
18. Radford, *Derby Works and Midland Locomotives.*
19. Rous Marten, 'Locomotive Practice & Performance'.
20. Ibid.
21. Tuplin, W. A., *Midland Steam.*
22. Cox, *Locomotive Panorama* Vol. 1.
23. Radford, *Derby Works and Midland Locomotives.*
24. Ibid.
25. Ibid.
26. *Grace's Guides*, quoted from the biography reprinted from the *Engineer* magazine.
27. Ibid.
28. Clayton, James, 'The Paget Locomotive', *Railway Gazette*, 2 November 1945.
29. Radford, *Derby Works and Midland Locomotives.*

30. Leech, 'Midland Railway 8-cylinder 2-6-2 No 2299'.
31. Ibid.
32. Tuplin, *Midland Steam.*
33. Clayton, 'The Paget Locomotive'.
34. Ibid., note appended to main article by editor.
35. Radford, *Derby Works and Midland Locomotives.*
36. Tuplin, *Midland Steam.*
37. Hamilton Ellis, *The Midland Railway.*
38. Today the boss's daughter would expect the job for herself, and why not?
39. Hamilton Ellis, *The Midland Railway.*
40. Leech, 'Midland Railway 8-cylinder 2-6-2 No 2299'.
41. Radford, *Derby Works and Midland Locomotives.*
42. Hamilton Ellis, *The Midland Railway.*
43. Tuplin, *Midland Steam.*
44. Powell, 'Living with LM Locomotives'.
45. Tuplin, *Midland Steam.*
46. Ibid.
47. Leech, 'Midland Railway 8-cylinder 2-6-2 No 2299'.
48. Powell, 'Living with LM Locomotives'.
49. Leech, 'Midland Railway 8-cylinder 2-6-2 No 2299'.
50. Clayton, 'The Paget Locomotive'.

Chapter 7

1. Chacksfield, J. E., *Richard Maunsell – An Engineering Biography.*
2. Ahrons, E. L., *Locomotive & Train Working in the Latter Part of the 19th Century* Volume 6.
3. Joynt, E. E., *Reminiscences of an Irish Locomotive Works* (accessed online via Steamindex)
4. Ibid.
5. Atkins, C. P., suggestion made in correspondence with the author.
6. Marx, K., *Wainwright and His Locomotives.*
7. Ibid.
8. Chacksfield, *Richard Maunsell.*
9. Holcroft, *Locomotive Adventure* Vol. 1.
10. It is to Holcroft that we are indebted for much of what we know about the background to SE&C and SR locomotive developments.

11. Bradley, *The Locomotive History of the South Eastern & Chatham Railway*.
12. Holcroft, *Locomotive Adventure* Vol. 1.
13. Bradley, *The Locomotive History of the South Eastern & Chatham Railway*.
14. Holcroft, *Locomotive Adventure* Vol. 1.
15. Ibid.
16. Bradley, *The Locomotive History of the South Eastern & Chatham Railway*.
17. Ibid.
18. Cox, *Locomotive Panorama* Vol. 1.
19. Bradley, D. L., *Locomotives of the LB&SCR* Part 3.
20. Hamilton Ellis, C., *The London Brighton & South Coast Railway*.
21. Holcroft, *Locomotive Adventure* Vol. 1.
22. Summers, L. A., *British Railways Steam 1948–1970*.
23. Forge, 'Eastleigh & Locomotive Design'.
24. Holcroft, *Locomotive Adventure* Vol. 1.
25. Hamilton Ellis, *The London Brighton & South Coast Railway*.
26. Elliott, Sir John, *On and Off the Rails*.
27. Ibid.
28. Holcroft, *Locomotive Adventure* Vol. 1.
29. Chacksfield, *Richard Maunsell*.
30. Cox, *Locomotive Panorama* Vol. 1.
31. Rolt, *Red for Danger*.
32. Bradley, *The Locomotive History of the South Eastern & Chatham Railway*.
33. This model is now in the possession of the Great Western Trust at Didcot Railway Centre and is sometimes on public exhibition.
34. Bradley, *The Locomotive History of the South Eastern & Chatham Railway*.
35. Summers, *British Railways Steam*.
36. Chacksfield, *Richard Maunsell*.
37. Nock, O. S., *British Locomotives of the 20th Century* Volume 1.
38. Holcroft, *Locomotive Adventure* Vol. 1.
39. Forge, 'Eastleigh & Locomotive Design'.

Chapter 8

1. Coombs, L. F. E., correspondence with the author, April 2016.
2. Bonavia, Michael, *History of the LNER*, 3 volumes.
3. Coombs, correspondence with the author, April 2016.
4. Ibid.

5. Hughes, Geoffrey, *Sir Nigel Gresley – The Engineer and His Family*.
6. Russell, O. W., 'Some Thoughts on Gresley's Derived Motion', *Back Track*, November/December 1990.
7. Bulleid, H. A. V., *Master Builders of Steam*.
8. Ibid.
9. Tuplin, W. A., *British Steam Since 1900*.
10. Bulleid, *Master Builders of Steam*.
11. Brown, F. A. S., *Sir Nigel Gresley: Locomotive Engineer*.
12. Phillipson, *Steam Locomotive Design, Data and Formulae*.
13. Brown, *Sir Nigel Gresley: Locomotive Engineer*.
14. Bulleid, *Master Builders of Steam*.
15. Allen, C. J., 'Locomotive Practice & Performance', *Railway Magazine*, 1936.
16. Bulleid, *Master Builders of Steam*.
17. Ibid.
18. Ibid
19. Ibid.
20. Brown, *Sir Nigel Gresley: Locomotive Engineer*.
21. Bulleid, *Master Builders of Steam*.
22. Russell, 'Some Thoughts on Gresley's Derived Motion'.
23. Gresley, H. N., 'The Three Cylinder High Pressure Locomotive', *Proc.IMechE*, 1925.
24. Bulleid, *Master Builders of Steam*.
25. Coombs, correspondence with the author, April 2016.
26. Russell, 'Some Thoughts on Gresley's Derived Motion'.
27. Holcroft, *Locomotive Adventure* Vol. 1.
28. Brown, *Sir Nigel Gresley: Locomotive Engineer*.
29. Holcroft, *Locomotive Adventure* Vol. 1.
30. Brown, *Sir Nigel Gresley: Locomotive Engineer*.
31. Bulleid, *Master Builders of Steam*.
32. Ibid.
33. Ibid.
34. Allen, C. J., *British Pacific Locomotives*.
35. Bruce, A. W., *The Steam Locomotive in America*.
36. Nock, O. S., *The Locomotives of Sir Nigel Gresley*.
37. *Hansard*, 12 May 1921.
38. RCTS, *Locomotives of the LNER* Part 1.
39. Bonavia, *History of the LNER*.

40. Ibid.

41. The GWR figures are quoted from the Financial Reports issued by the Board to the GWR's Annual General Meeting.

42. The LNER figures are quoted from the detailed abstracts of LNER Annual Financial Reports published in the *Railway Gazette*.

43. RCTS, *Locomotives of the LNER* Part 2a.

44. RCTS, *Locomotives of the LNER* Part 1.

45. Allen, *British Pacific Locomotives*.

46. RCTS, *Locomotives of the LNER*.

47. Cox, *Locomotive Panorama* Vol. 1.

48. Allen, *British Pacific Locomotives*.

49. Nock, O. S., *Speed Records on Britain's Railways*.

50. The reports of 100 mph ascribed to the GWR *City of Truro* and the LNER *Flying Scotsman* are not unassailable achievements.

51. Bonavia, *History of the LNER*.

52. Coombs, correspondence with the author, April 2016.

53. Tuffrey, P., *The Cock o'the North*.

54. Brown, *Sir Nigel Gresley: Locomotive Engineer*.

55. Chacksfield, *Sir William Stanier: A New Biography*.

56. Bonavia, *History of the LNER*.

Select Bibliography

Books

The following books have been quoted in the text. There will be others, general railway and locomotive studies. that will have supporting information to the details recorded here.

Ahrons, E. L., *The British Steam Locomotive 1825 – 1925*.
Ahrons, E. L., *Locomotive & Train Working in the Latter Part of the 19th Century*. Six volumes.
Allen, C. J., *British Pacific Locomotives*.
Allen, C. J., *British Atlantic Locomotives*.
Atkins, C. P., *The Scottish 4-6-0 Classes*.
Bird, G. F. and Christopher, John, *Locomotives of the Great Northern Railway*.
Bonavia, Michael, *History of the LNER*. Three volumes.
Bradley, D. L., *The Locomotive History of the South Eastern Railway*.
Bradley, D. L., *The Locomotive History of the South Eastern & Chatham Railway*.
Bradley, D. L., *Locomotives of the LB&SCR*.
Bradley, D. L., *The Locomotive History of the London, Chatham & Dover Railway*.
Brown, F. A. S., *Sir Nigel Gresley: Locomotive Engineer*.
Bruce, A. W., *The Steam Locomotive in America*.
Bulleid, H. A. V., *Master Builders of Steam*.
Chacksfield, J. E., *The Drummond Brothers: A Scottish Duo*.
Chacksfield, J. E., *Richard Maunsell – An Engineering Biography*.
Chacksfield, J. E., *Sir William Stanier: A New Biography*.
Chapelon, A., *Locomotive a Vapeur*.
Cormack, J. R. H. and Stevenson, J. L., *Highland Railway Locomotives*.
Cox, E. S., *Locomotive Panorama*. Two volumes.
Dendy Marshall, C. F. and Kidner, R. W., *A History of the Southern Railway*.

Dow, George, *Great Central*. Two volumes.

Elliott, Sir John, *On and Off the Rails*.

Gibbs, G. H. and Simmons, Jack (ed.), *The Birth of the Great Western Railway: Extracts from Gibbs Diary & Correspondence*.

Gibson, J. C., *GWR Locomotive Design, a Critical Survey*.

Glover, John, *Southern Electric* (New edn, 2001).

Gooch, Sir Daniel and Gooch, John (ed.), *The Diaries of Sir Daniel Gooch*.

Hamilton Ellis, C., *Some Classic Locomotives*.

Hamilton Ellis, C., *The South Western Railway: Its Mechanical History and Background, 1838–1922*.

Hamilton Ellis, C., *Twenty Locomotive Men*.

Hamilton Ellis, C., *Four Main Lines*.

Hamilton Ellis, C., *The Midland Railway*.

Hamilton Ellis, C., *The London Brighton & South Coast Railway*.

Highet, Campbell, *Scottish Locomotive History*.

Highet, Campbell, *The Glasgow & South Western Railway*.

Hills, R. L. and Patrick, D., *Beyer, Peacock: Locomotive Builders to the World*.

Holcroft, H., *Outline of Great Western Locomotive Practice*.

Holcroft, H., *The Armstrongs of the Great Western*.

Holcroft, H., *Locomotive Adventure*. Two volumes.

Hughes, Geoffrey, *Sir Nigel Gresley – The Engineer and His Family*.

Ingram, M. E., Hoole, K., Hinchliffe, B., *The Hull & Barnsley Railway*. Two volumes.

Johnson, J., and Long, R. A., *British Railways Engineering 1948–1980*.

Kidner, R. W., *The South Eastern Railway and the SE & CR*.

Leech, K. H. and Body, M. G., The Stirling Singles.

Lowe, James W., *British Steam Locomotive Builders*.

MacDermot, E. T. and Clinker, C. R., *History of the Great Western Railway*. Two volumes. A third volume has been added by O. S. Nock.

Marx, K., *Wainwright and His Locomotives*.

Middlemass, Tom: *The Scottish 4-4-0*.

Nock, O. S., *Speed Records on Britain's Railways*.

Nock, O. S., *The Railway Race to the North*.

Nock, O. S., *The Locomotives of Sir Nigel Gresley*.

Nock, O. S., *LNER Steam*.

Nock, O. S., *British Locomotives of the 20th Century*. Three volumes.

Nock, O. S., *Speed Records on Britain's Railways*.

Peck, A. S., *The Great Western at Swindon Works.*

Phillipson, E. A., *Steam Locomotive Design Data and Formulae.*

Radford, J. B., *Derby Works and Midland Locomotives.*

RCTS, *Locomotives of the LNER.* Several parts. This has no specifically named authors.

Rolt, L. T. C., *Brunel.*

Rolt, L. T. C., *Red for Danger.*

Rolt, L. T. C., *Patrick Stirling's Locomotives.*

Sharman, M., *The Crampton Locomotive.*

Shields, T. H., *The Evolution of Locomotive Valve Gears.*

Summers, L. A., *Swindon Steam: A New Light on GWR Loco Development.*

Summers, L. A., *British Railways Steam 1948–1970.*

Tuffrey, P., *The Cock o'the North.*

Tuplin, W. A., *Midland Steam.*

Tuplin, W. A., *British Steam Since 1900.*

Vaughan, A. H., *Isambard Kingdom Brunel: Engineering Knight Errant.*

Vaughan, A. H., *The Intemperate Engineer.*

Vaughan, A. H., *LTC Rolt: Myth-maker.*

Westwood, J. N., *Locomotive Designers in the Age of Steam.*

Articles in magazines references in this book

Allen, C. J., 'Locomotive Practice & Performance', *Railway Magazine*, 1936. (Allen wrote for the *Railway Magazine* from 1909 to the end of 1958.)

Anthony, Pierre, 'French Crampton type locomotives', *Locomotive Magazine*, October 1932.

Atkins, C. P., 'Richard Mountford Deeley: Author & Polymath', *Midland Record Society Journal*, 2004.

Baker, P. H., 'John Viret Gooch', *Back Track*, May 1995.

Clayton, James, 'The Paget Locomotive', *Railway Gazette*, 2 November 1945.

Forge, E. L., 'Eastleigh & Locomotive Design Part 1', *Railway World*, July 1983.

Forge, E. L., 'Eastleigh & Locomotive Design Part 2', *Railway World*, November 1983.

Leech, K. H., 'Midland Railway 8-cylinder 2-6-2 No 2299', *Railway Gazette*, 2 November 1945.

McKillop, N. (writing as Torem Beg), 'Highland Interlude', *Trains Illustrated*, August 1957.

Nisbet, A. F., 'The Attempt on the Life of James Stirling', *Back Track*.

Powell, A. J. (writing as '45671'), 'Living with LM Locomotives', *Trains Illustrated*,
   November 1957.
Rous Marten, C., 'Locomotive Practice & Performance', *Railway Magazine*,
   November 1903, January 1907. (Rous Marten wrote for the *Railway Magazine*
   from 1902 to 1908.)
Russell, O. W., 'Some Thoughts on Gresley's Derived Motion', *Back Track*,
   November/December 1990.

In addition to the above, the online *Grace's Guide* makes available many of the
biographies, usually obituaries, of locomotive engineers that appeared in the
Engineer magazine.

The Diaries of David Joy. The author is unsure whether a full version of this has
been published but there is a microfilmed copy of the original document held in the
Science Museum Library at Imperial College, London. This shows that the document
was, in fact, written towards the end of his life and was not, strictly, a diary.

Seymore Clarke's GWR Traffic Superintendent's Reports are available to
researchers at the National Archives, Kew.

The following papers read to the Institution of Mechanical and/or Civil Engineers
have been mentioned in the text:

Drummond, D., 'Particulars of the most recent parts of the London & South
   Western Railway company's Engines', *Proc.ICivE* 1897/8.
Crampton, T. R., 'Construction of Locomotive Engines', *Proc.ICivE* 1849.
Churchward, G. J., On Large Locomotive Boilers, *Proc.IMechE* 1906.
Gresley, H. N., 'The Three Cylinder High Pressure Locomotive', *Proc.IMechE*
   1925.

The following is not a railway journal but for those interested is a model of
genealogical research:

Deeley, R. M., *A Genealogical History of Montfort-Sur-Risle and Deeley of
   Halesown.*